LISTENING TO THE SAVAGE

Listening to the Savage

River Notes and Half-Heard Melodies

BARBARA HURD

The University of Georgia Press —— *Athens*

A **Wormsloe**
FOUNDATION
nature book

© 2016 by the University of Georgia Press
Athens, Georgia 30602
www.ugapress.org

Designed by Erin Kirk New
Set in Cycles
Printed and bound by Sheridan Books

The paper in this book meets the guidelines for
permanence and durability of the Committee on
Production Guidelines for Book Longevity of the
Council on Library Resources.

Most University of Georgia Press titles are
available from popular e-book vendors.

Printed in the United States of America
20   19   18   17   16   C   5   4   3   2   1

Library of Congress Cataloging-in-Publication Data

Hurd, Barbara.
    [Essays. Selections]
    Listening to the savage : river notes and half-heard melodies
/ Barbara Hurd.
    pages cm
    "A Wormsloe Foundation Nature Book."
    ISBN 978-0-8203-4895-7 (ebook) — ISBN 978-0-8203-4894-0
(hardcover : alk. paper)
    I. Title.
    PS3608.U766A6   2016
    814'.6—dc23   2015007733

for Caitlin, Samantha, Keva, and Asher

It is not sufficient any longer to listen at the end of a wire to the rustling of the galaxies.

LOREN EISELEY

Contents

Acknowledgments

Some of these essays, in one version or another, first appeared in other publications.

"The Ear Is a Lonely Hunter" was published in *Ecotone* (Fall 2015).

"Dissonance" first appeared in *The Sun* (May 2011).

"To Keep an Ear to the Ground" was originally published in the *Bellingham Review* 37, no. 68 (Spring 2014).

"A True Seer *Hears*" appeared first in *Fourth River* (Spring 2014).

"Listening to the Same River Twice" was originally published in *Prairie Schooner* (Spring 2014).

"Keys" was short-listed for the William Hazlitt Essay Prize 2013, London, England.

"Whose Story Is This?" was originally published in the *New Ohio Review* (Spring 2013).

The lines in "The Ear Is a Lonely Hunter" from Gerald Stern's poem "Frogs" are from *In Beauty Bright: Poems* by Gerald Stern, copyright © 2012 by Gerald Stern. Used by permission of W. W. Norton & Company, Inc.

Gratitude, always, to my husband, Stephen Dunn, for his discerning eye and to my agent, Cynthia Cannell, for her support and encouragement.

LISTENING TO THE SAVAGE

1

The Ear Is a Lonely Hunter

It is always in the belly that we end up listening, or start listening.
The ear opens onto the sonorous cave that we then become.
JEAN-LUC NANCY

For most of its life, a spadefoot toad listens only for rain. Buried several feet underground, metabolism slowed, it holes up for months. Above ground, winter and drought parch the land, coyotes battle possums, owls lift the unsuspecting rattler high into the air. The toad might hear, now and then, the overhead scurry of rodents, a sudden whoosh of raptor wings. But deep in its burrow, out of sight, it doesn't fret about predators' hunger and barely listens to the various sounds of eat-or-be-eaten. Interested in only one sound—the patter of raindrops—it can wait for months, even years.

Imagine the scene. Without water or food, relying on its skin to suck a bit of moisture from surrounding soil, it half-dozes until at last a first raindrop pings onto the hard-baked crust above. The toad's tympanic membranes—small, unprotected patches of skin behind the eyeballs—begin to vibrate. Stirring from its stupor, it might hear that ping as a light knock on the ceiling, turn its bumpy head in the burrow, and listen for another.

These are things I sometimes think about at night when I'm standing at the edge of the Savage River in western Maryland and some blanket of hush has begun to descend: beings in their burrows, the kinds of alarms that alert, the fact that we, human and toad alike, are roused from sleep and other lethargies by sound more often than by sight, inklings—if this were a more comic-book world—that the eyes would have feet; the ears, hands. One sense travels; the other receives. The first is a river; the other, a pond.

The eye, German philosopher Lorenz Oken says, *takes a person into the world. The ear brings the world into a human being.* Ask Helen Keller if, forced to choose, she'd rather restore her vision or her hearing.

If, as the ancients say, careful seeing can deepen the world, then careful listening might draw it more nigh. The eyes, after all, can close at will; we can avert a glance, lower the gaze, look elsewhere. But the ears, these entrances high on our bodies, doubled, corniced, aimed in opposite directions, can do nothing but remain helplessly open. And when some unexpected sound enters, then our bodies, like the toad's, go on high alert, and our minds, our sometimes irrepressible, untoad-like minds, go into high gear.

———

At least that's what happened one morning when my five-year-old granddaughter Samantha and I stopped at a farm to buy broccoli and heard a sound that didn't seem to belong. It wasn't the grating whir of a deep-shale drill—though I fear that's coming—but a tortured kind of screech. She cupped her hands to her ears, turned one way and the other, and then we heard it again: one long, mournful cry among the otherwise bucolic sounds of a small farm. It was like one of those puzzles from kindergarten: three circles and a triangle and your job was to mark the one that's different. Only these weren't visual images that day; they were sounds, and they didn't line up neatly. They came, instead, from various corners of the farm: one familiar low clang from the pasture, one deep galumph from the west, a light rustle overhead, and as soon as we'd stepped from the car, that lone, chilling cry from beyond the barn.

From the Latin word *monere,* meaning *to warn,* have come *divine omen, evil omen, warning, misshapen deliverer of bad news, monster, to admonish.* And finally, *to summon.*

Though it haunted, the puzzling sound in the farmyard was not yet a summons, at least not in the way trumpets might have summoned the faithful in Old Testament times or the way, some say, certain mantras might summon ancestors or angels. It did not draw Samantha to it so much as it drew from her an imaginative response: a big frog with a cold? Dragon with a sore throat? *Summon up* might be the better term, as in *to rouse* or *to call to mind*.

Samantha is slender and pale, an undercooked wood sprite with a cascade of copper hair and a sprightly mind that somersaults and spins. She once told me, apropos of nothing, "When crocodiles climb trees, they wear their yellow boots." Another time: "I like the people best who fall down." Her eyes are blue and warm or angry or impish. Sometimes I catch her, bent over her arm, tracing the blue veins beneath her almost translucent skin.

We were a few miles that day from my home in the mountains of western Maryland, where she visits me often and where we often visit the Savage River, which slips from Finzel Swamp and flows south through farmland and forest before dumping into the Potomac River. Downstate, not far from where Samantha lives, the Potomac is broad and dirtied; by the time it gets to our nation's capital, its banks host a lineup of gleaming memorials—to Lincoln, to Jefferson, to veterans of foreign wars. But up here in the mountains, the Savage—clear and cold—is a secluded tributary or, as I like to think of it, a place to which tribute might be brought. And so I bring her often. I don't know what homage we're making, what gift from us could possibly matter to the wildness all around. We come anyway, to crouch on the banks or wade in; sometimes we listen for fish splashing, chipmunks among the hemlocks; sometimes she's content to turn over rocks.

The source of light rustle was easy, she said that day on the farm: wind in the trees. Low clang was simple too, once the cow ambled toward us, her thick neck swaying the clapper on the bell. And though we circled the reedy pond twice and never saw the bullfrog, its galumph was familiar enough to be, for the moment, uninteresting.

Ten minutes passed. We closed our eyes and listened to more cowbells, the scratch of hoe in the garden, a banging door, and a different plunk in the pond. And then, from somewhere behind the barn, *aye-aw, aye-aw,* that harsh and mournful cry again. Back up the lane we meandered until, another fifteen minutes later, it came from another direction, beyond the herb garden.

Ears are tethered—sometimes tediously so—to heads. We can no more send them off on scouting missions, like radar-equipped boomerangs, than we can commission our eyes to sally forth without us and bring back the visual news. The body must plod along, dragging our history and our longings. We're a lumbering posse of investigation rolling up and down the farm lanes, maybe wanting new sounds to sound like old sounds, so long as the old sounds sound like solace, the wish for which we drag along too. No wonder the comfort of handed-down stories.

But the ear, fixed to the head, seems, at times, unfixed to the brain, so that seemingly unfettered sound provides no comfort, seems, instead, to bypass the ears' intricate ties to the mind and plummet directly to the belly. Especially if it's a mournful sound, it can live for years in there, siphoning from the belly's storehouse of unfinished business other unidentified sounds, composing whole arias of longing. Such a belly can become a refuge. Such a sound can both imprison and relieve.

Can we make it otherwise? And should we?

When I was nine, my favorite hymn included the lines,

> and to my listening ears
> all nature sings and round me rings
> the music of the spheres.

In high school, I listened to Lord Byron: *A Truth . . . it is a tone, / the sound and source of music.*

In college, Thoreau: *All sound . . . a vibration of the universal lyre.*

Years later, for Pythagoras's celestial music, Kepler's planetary pitches, Rilke's *unheard starry music.*

I loved the Eastern notion of listening to the world as vibration. How marvelous, I thought back then, all this fitting together, this symphony of sound. I listened only for harmony, coherence, which is another way of saying reassurance, and knew nothing at that point of the roar of floodwaters or tornadoes.

That morning, Samantha, forehead furrowed, listened only for the source of that mournful cry, which sounded, too, like *Allah, Allah* or *help, help.*

———

Meanwhile, the spadefoot toad, which cannot, of course, hear the sound of any human longing, has been alerted by rain. As the patter above begins to quicken, so does its heart, its blood. Its four-toed feet begin to claw the sides of its burrow.

———

A few pings might alert; a pattern might even summon. For good or for ill, it can be like this for us at times too. A sound—a word? a bugle cry?—begins as a stray note, a single *come hither* that soon becomes a chord and then a marching song, and suddenly we're off, following what appears to be a drum major with a plan designed to out-thrum any hesitations. How many of us have listened to our own recurring dreams, reheard them as subpoenas, acted on what we swore was the destiny we could access only in unconscious states?

In my mid-thirties, I had a series of dreams in which an unseen person stood in my yard at night and played the harmonica. In the dream, if I turned on the porch light, he disappeared. If I crept out the back door and kept my eyes shut, I could approach.

But there's this bedeviling detail about a sound that seems to summon: there's no rewind button. A change in the visual field alerts us; such a sight can usually be stared at, contemplated, scanned again, and reconsidered. A single sound can alert us too, but there's no way to restudy what has, in an instant, swooped through the ear canal, brushed against tympanic membranes, and set those tiny bones astirring. The sound gets lodged in the imagination—or, as Jean-Luc Nancy says, in the belly—and can become who we then become or become the unsaid thing we listen to again and again. Think of Joan of Arc. Think of any number of murderers obeying the sounds they claim to have heard. The problem with hearing such sounds as a summons is that they often won't bear scrutiny. That is their power too.

I never told that dream to my now ex-husband, who spent those fitful months trying to sleep beside me. How do you say to a person who matters, *I have to go now; the music has summoned me?* How do you even say such things to yourself?

"Some dreams," Samantha, standing up in her booster seat, once told her mother, "some dreams you tell and some you don't."

———

The toad's job is simpler. When raindrops become rainfall, it makes its slow way up the burrow it might not have left for years—the record is a decade—and emerges into wet night. It is not the only creature on high alert. Every toad-hungry predator around knows that rain means that food is about to climb right out of the earth—manna from below—and it's ready, its eyes tracking movement, its nose catching whiffs.

The toads begin to call in their croaky voices; the voices lead them to one another, begin to synchronize, become choir-like. This is, of course, about mating, but it's also about the chorus of sound blurring the voice of a solitary toad. An owl can't pinpoint the singular target within a throng. A coyote won't pounce on a swarm. For the toads congregating in vernal pools, acoustical camaraderie is a first line of defense.

———

Acoustical camaraderie is not what I meant by *music of the spheres*. What I think I meant was planetary harmonies, the romantic notion that the universe resounds, that love has to do with vibrating octaves and the hills are alive with the sound of music. All that.

When I retired, I bought a sleeping bag for starry nights, not for the chance to hear any universal lyre, but for the chance to hear all this: barred owls, predawn peepers, huff of black bear in the cornfield. And when the occasional reward—three huffs, scores of deer snorts, the cackle and cluck of wild turkey, and twice, the midnight yip of coyote—thrilled but failed to satisfy, I found myself calling the area's most formidable piano teacher and signing up for lessons.

Which is how I came to be sitting, weeks later, on a stool in front of her piano, clunking my way through a simple Mozart sonata, when out the corner of my eyes I saw her right hand rise from her lap and float toward me. I leaned toward the score: D-sharp, D-sharp, why couldn't I hit that right and why couldn't the music that flows through her hands just keep flowing, right into mine? And then there was her hand on mine, moving it—moving it!— sideways so that my index finger hit that D-sharp, and then her hand floated back to her lap, and I played the right note—yes—but it was the assumed right-to-touch, to press and lift, to move parts of my body around that jolted me, her implied *Allow me. This will help you to hear what you want to hear, this will bring the music into the body.* She touches my shoulders—relax! My back—up straight! My wrists, she makes them undulate—loosen up! Is it true that the world—or, in this case, music—cannot enter a rigid body? That it's not just our ears that must be open but also our joints, our chests, our lungs, our pores, our hearts? *And here, hear this?* I close my eyes. She plays a tonic chord and wants me to hear how it suggests home.

I love that Betty talks to me like this, as if she believes I have a chance at understanding. Maybe I will, someday. Maybe it will seep in, right through my fingers, my skin. But right now, a lot of what she says is as if in a foreign tongue, as if we're at some café table in an exotic country, and she's leaning toward me, those blue eyes not just clear but warm, her face lit up, and out of her mouth come impassioned words she so wants me to understand. Diatonic, tonic, andante. Sometimes I nod my head just to keep her talking. Sometimes I just sit there, immobilized by ignorance I hope to hide from her, though I know she sees right through my pose. Even that doesn't stop her.

"Hear this," she says, "the way those three notes play off the major chord?" Her fingers skim across a few keys, and we're back in her living room, the Steinway in front of us like a large black window I want to fall through, whose secrets, on some days, I think I'd give anything for.

A year into weekly lessons, I began to have some vague sense that I might someday get an inkling of the underlying structures, the extraordinary complexity that underlies music. The Greeks, she says, figured a lot of this out, and much of it has to do with vibrations. Is she, too, talking about the music of the spheres?

Nine months after that, I realized I had no idea how to touch a piano key. I'd been walking along the river after two days of rain, feeling the way my sneakered foot pressed into the wet duff of the forest floor, watching the way my heel sank first, remembering that a tracking expert once taught me to lower the toe first, better to control pressure and balance. Do I touch a piano key like a hammer lowered on a hammer? Or a boat nudging into the dock? Or a bird alighting on a branch?

Play, she reminds me, as if you were reentering the piece anew each time. Or play as if you were Mozart, creating each measure for the first time, exploring where the next note should go, a toe inching forward over uncertain ground, finding the best foothold, which might not be the third but the fifth or a sudden minor chord, the trees suddenly aleaf, the clouds lowering. Play as if your ear were the creator.

Meanwhile, on that farm, Samantha kept imagining the source of the odd sound—'Not a horse," she declared, "maybe Eeyore?"—and the bullfrog hiding in the reeds continued to galumph.

"Ever see one do that?" I asked her. She shook her head. I stood behind her and placed my hand on the front of her neck. "Breathe in," I told her, "and as you breathe out, hum, and imagine your neck swelling so much that it pushes my hand out, like this." I made my hand into a cup that billowed away from her neck, out past her chin. As she let loose a quick hum, she rolled her eyes downward, trying to see my hand as it seemed to blow up with her breath.

"That's what a frog does, only it's a pouch in his own neck that he blows up." I gently stretched her skin away from her throat. "Like this. That's what makes his croak so loud." And right on time, the bullfrog galumphed a big one, and Samantha pushed my hand away and giggled, and though I was tempted to recite to her a few lines from a Gerald Stern poem titled, "Frogs," I restrained myself. What, after all, would she make of them?

> Think of the music on a summer night
> with no one conducting and think of how warm it might be
> and how love songs may have gotten started there.

Started there, in a pond among rattling cattails, right there, at our feet.

Which makes Byron's notions of *Truth . . . the sound and source of music* seem chillingly distant now, way too fashioned and arch, some kind of cosmic hearsay arising out of a wish to be elsewhere. What was, what is, this ancient yearning upward for celestial harmony? Do we think it might drown out the discord here on earth?

Here's my prayer: Help us to listen to the sounds—fragmented, atonal, melodic, diminished, augmented—of our own lives and of the myriad lives among us: cricket trill, beaver whack, birdsong, snake hiss, donkey bray. Give me the voiced morsels of this child ("Meemi, sometimes I get dark messages from my eyes"), unconducted love songs begun in the cattaily edges of a pond and the bellowy burp of bullfrogs. For this is the grounding, the sounding, things as they are, for now and for now. Amen.

—

On a hike along the coast of Maine, I listened to rain that splatted on the broad leaves of alder or birch, splatted louder than when it slalomed through spruce needles. Closing my eyes, I realized I could tell from the sound of the rain which tree I was walking toward. Something about that cheered me: sound conjures image, which divides into needle or leaf. Textures deepen; forms multiply.

For other cultures, of course, such discernments are a matter of survival. That howl in the distance: coyote or wolf? And those twig snaps up ahead: deer or bear with a couple of cubs? But for many of us who lock our doors at night and buy meat at the market, such distinctions have, for perhaps hundreds of years, begun to blur, even to seem irrelevant. There's a certain relief in that—constant vigilance takes a toll—but also a certain loss: a finely tuned sense of the natural world recedes, perhaps beyond retrieval.

When rain became downpour, I retreated to my cabin, where in midafternoon I had to turn on the lamp just to see the book on the bed. The rain sounded like brush against a snare drum of a roof: unordered thrum, unshaped. I changed into dry clothes, checked for leaks in the ceiling, put Mozart's Sonata in C—learning to play it is taking me months—in the CD player and cranked up the sound. The notes, discrete and arranged, filled the cabin.

Spinning the volume up and down, I pitted Mozart against deluge, back and forth between downpour and upwelling, between wet muffling and clear arpeggios, until it was the interplay between Mozart and rain, between musical genius and the mundanity of *this* world—not any harmonic music of the spheres, those cold and distant planets—that moved me.

If there were spadefoot toads in that part of Maine that rainy afternoon, there'd have been an explosion of croaks outside my cabin, a melee of mating. The coyote and owl would have gone on high alert. Outside, the mushrooms—*collared earthstars*—must have been pushing their delicate bodies up through dampened humus. Attached to them and hidden below, the mycelium—the vast interconnected, thread-like tubes—can spread a hundred feet, form their own versions of underground galaxies. Whatever sounds they make are unconducted; real intimacy, after all, makes a conductor obsolete.

———

I don't know how often I've been looking when I should have been listening. *Allah, Allah. Help, help.* We hear what we need to hear. Isn't this the hidden meaning of a summons?

"It's a peacock," the farmer told Samantha. "Someone brought it here years ago."

"A peacock? Huh? Like in the zoo?" she asked, scrunching her face.

I confess I didn't want her to know. I wanted her to remember that day as the day she heard a sound that didn't belong, a not-knowing she might make room for somewhere in the imagination that vibrates between belly and mind. Let there be summonses you can't jump to, I want to tell her; the richest ones might not be followable for decades. Let there be room for what you might someday become.

———

From the Latin word *monere* has also come *monitor*, which is one reason I wander along the Savage River so often. I'm a volunteer for the local watershed association, and after gathering samples and recording data, I've taken to meandering up- and downstream from our monitoring sites. Sometimes Samantha's with me; more often I'm alone. For years I've watched for small excitements there—rummaging raccoons or a black bear in the water. I believed for so long that to pray was to pay attention, and by that I never thought to mean anything other than to see. But vision, I'm coming to understand, is deepened by listening, especially if the ear has turned from any wishful music of the spheres and heard, as if for the first time, the whoosh of wind in the trees or the cry of a red-tailed hawk.

Hearing, Helen Keller decided. *I'd want my hearing restored.*

I'm grateful, of course, not to have to choose and have no wish to downplay the importance of vision. But I want to think for a while about what might happen when myths—symphonic and enduring—begin to diminish and the ear learns to listen to what begat them in the first place, when listening becomes not just an inciter of desire but a way of paying tribute to where we are, to peepers and odd mournings, rain, Mozart, the lovely quirkiness of Samantha's mind—reasons, all of them, to turn my ear, that lonely hunter, and put it closer to the ground.

2

For the Record

When I hear music, I fear no danger.

HENRY DAVID THOREAU

Oh, Henry. Really? No danger at all? What about the belching smokestacks of nearby Lowell? The steam-spewing, snorting railroad that bordered Walden Pond?

And were you alive today, what about water pollution, habitat destruction? Would you ease your worries about them with a little Mozart on your music box or your flute out in the rowboat once again?

For the record: I'm a Thoreau fan. I find in his writing some of the most well-made sentences and thoughtful musings about the ploys of skunk cabbage, the point of having visitors, the epidemics of desperation. When I was a child, I might have agreed with him about music; listening to church hymns, I wouldn't have been thinking about danger or fear. But then, I probably wouldn't have been thinking about such things anyway, music or no music. Such was the nature of my childhood. Given that craggy face, though, I never imagined his as so innocent.

But this is not another essay about Thoreau. I wish, instead, to speak a word for worry, for focused consternation, and for water striders whose sexual antics (*pay attention*, Henry) include using a slender leg or two to ripple the surface of a quiet pond.

There's an art to worry. It begins with fashioning a concern to fit its subject, with bending the angst to conform to the scope of the trouble. I'm not interested in the worries of calamity howlers; they have little sense of proportion and probabilities, and most of their dire predictions seem backlit by a love of drama. Nor am I interested in the low-level, diffused anxieties like those of a friend of ours who once accused my second husband of underworry. That friend's worries take the form of heavy sighs. He worries about my husband's underworry, he says, sighing.

I value the quiet worriers, the ones whose furrowed brows make them attentive to whatever is a little off. Or might be. Maybe not now, but probably in the near future. The ones like my friend Terry, who knows the names of what concerns him: garlic mustard, he says, pointing to an invasive species that can choke out native herbs. And an algae charmingly called rock snot, which can smother river-bottom food supplies and habitat. We're in the Savage River one day in May when recent downpours have churned the current. The mountains rise steeply above us on either side of this deep-cut valley. It is, for us, for many, a haven of cool shadows, fast water, wilderness all around. Thoreau would have loved this place.

Terry had parked the car on a skinny stretch of shoulder, and we'd scrambled down the bank, inched our way into the river, knee deep here and rock strewn, toting plastic cups for water sampling. Concerned about warming waters, chemical spills, invasive species, and habitat destruction, we are part of a team of citizen monitors who patrol this so-far pristine river. We're out here all year long, up and down the twenty-nine miles of the river, taking samples, recording numbers, making observations about water clarity, flow, levels. Worried mostly about fracking, we're collecting baseline data—dissolved solids, conductivity, and temperatures—in case Maryland lifts the moratorium that has, so far, kept the trucks and wells and drills and slick water from contaminating the watershed.

Back on the bank a few minutes later, Terry and I log the data, clean equipment with distilled water and saline solutions, carry it back to the car, and look at each other. I don't remember which one of us says it first, but the agreement is mutual: river sounds get us going.

If the water weren't so high, he'd be after brook trout. "I'll hike," he says. "And you?"

"I'm after the Jesus bug," I say.

Terry, who has little tolerance for evangelicals, raises his eyebrows, wishes me luck. Leaving his fishing gear in the car, he heads up a nearby trail, while I inch my way down the bank and back along the river. There's a spot fifty yards or so upstream where the river has cut a quiet side channel, and that's where I head first.

Twenty minutes later, I'm stretched out by a fern-edged pool, watching a half dozen of them skitter across the water. Like all insects, they have six legs—in this case, two for grasping prey, two for rowing, two for steering, the latter four of which also work to keep their half-inch bodies hoisted just above the water's surface. Hence the "Jesus bug." "Skater insects," Thoreau called them. Water striders, Terry would say. With their four splayed legs, they can distribute their bit of weight across the delicate membrane that is the water's surface tension. Picture a kid too far out on thin ice on his belly, extending his four limbs, lying spread-eagled and still, until help arrives. Or picture a pontoon boat with four bumpers akin to the bug's waterproofed, air-pocketed legs. Even if a sudden ripple approaches, the strider can ride it, keep its body dry by floating up and down as the ripple passes underneath.

This is the kind of stuff Thoreau would have loved—all the details about clingy water molecules and surface tension and the hydrofuge hairs that line the insect's body. And maybe it's the kind of sight—quiet pool, no humans around, bugs walking on water—that prompted him to say about a piece of music, *In the light of this strain there is no thou nor I. We are actually lifted above ourselves.* I'm reminded of how, for years, I'd tried to imagine us, in whatever village, city, or nation, listening for that music, off in the celestial distance, that might help lift us out of our little lives, resolve our differences, lead us into some harmonious happily-ever-after.

If only, Henry, I hadn't grown skeptical of your "Universal lyre." If only I hadn't started to worry about the dangers of illusion, the futility of aiming for afterlives.

For the record: I am not by nature a worrier. In general, I like Thoreau's counsel about good lives not being troubled by ennui. And I like the wisdom of the baseball player who, asked if he worried about being traded, replied, "There's no use worrying about things you can't control because if you can't control them there's no use worrying about them." But isn't the real dilemma how to distinguish between what we can't control and what we can? Between coastal storm surges, for example, versus ozone holes? Asteroids versus invasive species?

Worries, for the moment, aside, it's the striders' dimpling I want to watch today, those long legs deliberately tapping on the water, creating what Thoreau, watching them on Walden Pond, called the *finest imaginable sparkle*. It's not sparkles, though, that I end up watching, but the underwater shadows they make. It takes a deliberate refocusing to see them and not the bug itself, but there they are, quick-darting blobs of dark gray, each of them rimmed with light, sliding and twitching on the river bottom. Perhaps it's the worrier in me that keeps looking below, eyeing shadows, anticipating trouble. Those legs, I know, do more than keep the body dry and fed. They also connive, which, for a female strider, can cause some consternation. There's a reason, after all, that a male climbing her back starts to thrum the water if she resists him, and the reason has nothing to do with upping her ardor. Thrumming, she knows, can summon the hungry backswimmer—Notonectidae— who, idling around in the same quiet pool, waits for that vibration. Sensing it, the backswimmer paddles closer. If the strider keeps up her squirming and the male climbing her back keeps up his leg-tapping, then the backswimmer, summoned, will grab her belly. It'll be all over in a second. For her, it's sometimes either sex or death. Is that Thoreau meant when he said, *The thrills of joy and thrills of pain are indistinguishable*? But isn't that part of our job? To worry those thrills apart, learn to enjoy one and protect ourselves from the other?

———

The ear, Nietzsche says, *is the organ of fear.* Putting that ear to the ground is akin to the strider sensing vibrations in the water, the spider sensing movement in its web. Something's always jiggling the water, the web. Food? Mate? Or foe? Agent of extortion? When unusual readings show up in our stream data, we want to know what invisible jiggling's going on. Sometimes it's all we have—tracings of disturbance, change in the ripples, warmer temperatures, more glint of sun—to tell us something new is under way. Music aside, Henry, this, I sometimes think, is the work of worrying river monitors—we extend our feelers, try to tune them to the many vibrations of the web—dissolved particles, changed conductivity readings, warmer temperatures. We're trying to hear an ecological pulse.

It would be tempting to say something about that familiar Chief Seattle quote, the one about all things being connected and what we do to the web we do to ourselves. But my interest here is less in unity, more in learning to detect warnings. How to decide which worries are worth worrying about, which not. And which worries are worth doing something about, which not.

In case and *what if* are the worriers' favorite phrases. In Pennsylvania, they're past *in case,* past *what if.* The waters around Dimock are already laced with methane. Here in Maryland, we're trying to translate those phrases into action—*dip, measure, record, observe, alert*—because for many of us that ear Nietzsche described already hears drills in the distance, the whine of chain saws, the spit of gravel from too many trucks on backcountry roads. The day that conductivity readings spike we might not have noticed any visible change in the river, still rippling along its deep and shadowy valley, still surface-skitted by water striders. But that spike will sound the early warning system. We'll know that somehow, somewhere, something foreign might be getting into the water. We'll be better ready to ramp up the resistance.

———

Water strider, skater insect, Jesus bug—no matter what you call them, they're engineered not to break the surface tension. We, however, seem to be. Consciousness means we have to worry about what's underground (literally and figuratively), what's making unexplained ripples, what's likely ahead. Or might be, if not now, then soon. Here along the river, the woods appear healthy, but we know from the white dabs on the hemlocks and the light smatter-ing of dropping needles that these trees are in trouble, infected by woolly adelgids and likely to die in several years. And we know that dead hemlocks means decreased shadows on the river, which means that temperatures will rise and brook trout will likely head even further upstream.

On my belly, I watch the striders and try to imagine what prompted Thoreau, raising his flute to his lips, to claim that music helped him become *adequate to any deed*.

Really? *Any* deed?

I wish Thoreau were right. I suspect he's wrong. I worry that it's lack of worry about what we've been doing that's helped cause the problems we have to worry about now.

For the record, Henry, I'm not really worried about your rec-ommending allaying fears through musical bliss. You're the one, after all, who made the famous observation about our lives of quiet desperation, and you're the one who later said the lines that have become my monitoring theme song: *You would fain devote yourself to the melody but you will hear more of it if you devote yourself to the work.*

My husband, the nonworrier, wonders what good such work will ultimately do. So do I, only I do more than wonder. I worry. And Thoreau's comment about music and fear aside, nothing eases worry like the sound of a river and the physical act of *doing* some-thing—weeding out invasive species, planting red spruce seedlings, monitoring the river, noting water striders like these as they dimple a glassy surface. If they disappear from pools like this one where I'm lying on my belly, that, too, will likely mean the water's grown too warm.

Ah, Henry, I'll wager that you, scribbling notes in your cabin by the pond, never worried about the difficulty scientists might have reading your atrocious handwriting some 150 years later. How could you have known they'd unearth those notebooks, use your records of 1850's bloom time to compare with ours today? To sound the alarm about Walden warming? But were you alive today and ambling about your pond, I'd wager you'd notice what's already a little off: blueberries and trillium in flower and maples aleaf more than two weeks early. You'd know that means earlier caterpillars, which means decreased food for the birds who can't resynch their calendars and migrate north while food is still being served, which means, among other things, that veery's song you loved to listen to (*vee-ur, veer*) might grow increasingly rare.

I suspect you'd worry if that happened.

Me too.

For the record: I'm not a pessimist. But easy optimism has given way to dogged hope. Like you, I'm listening to a lot of things, including the doleful wailings of screech owls. The tips of the water strider's feet are feathered. Hope might be too, but good worry is not. It's clad in work boots.

3

Mile 2

———————

"No," Samantha insists, stomping her foot, "not once have I ever been bossy. Not once in my whole tiny life."

She loves to guess a story's ending. So do I. About *Boy with the Big Foot*, she says, "I knew it! I just knew the kid wouldn't step on that ant."

———————

Like a churning river, certainties travel fast, can make a lot of noise. What matters most is the phrase that follows "certainties": *therefore* or *but*? And maybe the question of how to hear the story of a place like this where agitated ripples of a tributary are about to spill into the bigger river's quiet.

———————

My mother used to say the mourning dove's song was enough to wake the dead. But here where the Savage roars into the Potomac, the dove's perched on a branch, silently opening its beak, as if it's miming her version of mourning.

———————

Meanwhile, catfish smack their lips like suction cups against rocks in a torrent, a clinging kiss to keep themselves from being swept away, like the click and whir of hooks and silk secretions insects use to anchor themselves in a fast current. Others just get swept along.

Every river, of course, must disappear into the next largest one.

4

Dissonance

Do you not know that our soul is composed of harmony?

LEONARDO DA VINCI

Da Vinci's notion is such a nice notion that it's most likely wrong. Nice ideas, after all, are often inaccurate, too tidy or balanced to get at the harder truths about how we really live our lives. Surely the soul, if there is such a thing, is not composed just of harmonies but of discord and dissonance too. Nudged into consciousness by friction with the world, the soul, if I might continue the musical metaphor, likely plays more than a single melodic line. It shifts between major and minor keys, alters the phrasing, moves from soft to loud and back again, all over the course of a single lifetime, or day by day, maybe minute by minute. Perhaps it even feels simultaneously young and old, independent and needy, sanguine and depressed—a whole range of competing and contradictory emotions that, if we acknowledge them all, can leave us paralyzed, or on our way to becoming more fully human.

But I could be wrong. After all, it wasn't until I started piano lessons that I learned how much of my thinking about harmony and dissonance had been woefully undeveloped.

I used to think of dissonance as the clang of garbage-can lids on a windy street, someone's toady gratitude for a thoughtless gift, the small squirrel in the barred owl's beak, terms of endearment delivered with disdain. In a more conventional way, I thought I heard it just a few weeks ago when I sat on the piano bench next to my teacher, my left hand playing A, D, C, D; the right on D, C,

B, C. What I was hearing sounded wrong, a grotesque chimera of sound. I looked at my teacher with a question in my eyes, wondering whether this was Mozart's mistake or mine.

We were, as usual, in her home, seated at her Steinway, some months after my first lesson in more than fifty years and just eight months before my first scheduled performance of this piece. I have the long, thin fingers of a pianist, an old longing to play well, and, I've discovered, no talent whatsoever. She's an eighty-five-year-old, six-foot-tall, Juilliard-trained musician, legendary among her pupils for her insistence that music must be felt and drills must be practiced and for her relentless command, "Thumb under. Thumb *under.*" I hear her instructions, and I don't. Even now, months later, I'm still trying to train that lumpish left thumb and thinking more about all that I don't know.

—⁓—

A few weeks ago my daughter and I stood barefoot on a lakeshore not far from the Savage River, watching a small flock of geese out on the water. We'd come to the valley soon after Sunday breakfast with Samantha and her older sister, Caitlin, and no binoculars, planning on nothing more than skipping stones into the water before they started their drive back downstate. Squinting at the far-off flock, I wondered aloud whether the geese were merely passing through or wintering over. Caitlin plopped another rock into the water, and Samantha picked at the dirt between her toes, when a sudden sound alerted us, pulsing from somewhere so close I expected my hair to flutter the way my heart did.

Tara stepped toward her younger daughter, and Caitlin moved toward me, and I was suddenly back on a beach in Virginia forty years earlier when a solar eclipse had sent wave after wave of shadow across the sand, and all of us who'd come to see it felt like primitives, ready to appease the gods we'd recently dismissed as myth.

There it was again: that out-of-nowhere intrusion of discord so precipitously close I wanted to fling invisible things off my skin, until Caitlin tilted her head back, and then we all did—and instinctively ducked as dozens of geese pumped the air just twenty feet over our heads, swooping across the lake until they braked with their wings and splash-glided feet first into the water with the rest of the flock and everything went quiet.

It all happened so fast that there was no pausing, no musing about whether something was discordant or merely unexpected. It wasn't until I sat down with that dissonant measure in the Mozart sonata that I thought again about that disruption of a tranquil scene. It had jolted us, for sure, but was it a moment of dissonance or something else?

———

Dissonant sounds, Schoenberg claims, have a more *remote relationship to the occasional center*. Before taking piano lessons, I'd have said that dissonance feels more like there are suddenly *two* centers and they're anything but remote. Their collision, in fact, feels imminent, which is why we have that urge to swerve, to do anything but continue on with two notes, two centers, two beliefs on the verge of impact. The dissonance I thought I knew doesn't invite dawdling. In its midst, one lurches toward safety—or, if you're a beginning piano player like me, hurries into the next measure.

"No," my teacher said. "Try it again. And this time, *listen*." And there it was, again, that grating in the first measure. Yes, she nodded, that's right. I let my fingers linger there a few seconds, feeling the clash between those notes, trying to quell the urge to correct it. *This* is music?

———

I'm an obvious novice at the piano, and on those many days when I can't hear the music in my head, can't get my fingers to do what I want them to do, can't do much at all but bang at the keys and snort at myself, I sometimes give up and take off with my dog, Kassi, to the river, where a fast walk and a little stick-throwing will settle my nerves. Kassi's a rescued pup—a supposed yellow Lab–golden retriever mix who turned out to be all white and oblivious to dissonance, except perhaps when a deer bolts across the trail and she, wanting only to chase, hears an uncharacteristic sharpness in my command to come, come *now*. On a recent afternoon not long after the geese had startled the kids and me at the lake, Kassi and I meandered along the river to a place where for months I had been hearing the elongated screech of a tree creaking, even on windless days—a clear raspy bray somewhere between distressed cat and the swaying mast of an old clipper ship. The first time I heard it, last spring, I'd frozen, my eyes scanning the woods ahead for a wounded kitten or deer, even—ridiculous as this sounds—an abandoned baby. It's not your typical tree moaning in the wind, but something more solitary, plaintive, and unsettling.

Tree creaks are common, of course, in any woods, the result of friction within or between the trunks and branches. Internal friction results from the mish-mash of young and old fibers. The older fibers have begun to stiffen and dry; the younger ones remain supple. When a breeze sets a tree swaying, those fibers don't respond the same way. Some bend; some resist. Picture dancers on a stage, some ninety years old, some six. When the music begins, and they start to move, the younger ones—bouncy and lithe—will inevitably bump into the elders, who may be just trying to keep their balance, perhaps tap the foot less hobbled by arthritis. In a tree, such rubbing of young fiber against old sets off cracks and groans.

Or the discord can arise between trees, when one has grown too close to another or when disease or mortality has felled one, which, uprooted or splintered, starts its slow descent to the ground through the tangled mesh of surrounding branches. Many get caught middrop and languish in tilted postures for years, their bark rubbing against another's. This is no gentle grazing. An eighty-foot hemlock can weigh more than four thousand pounds. When it falls against a nearby oak and gets lodged in its branches, it bears down; it grinds. A slight breeze sets off a muffled fuss of squeaks and low-pitched muttering. There are days in an Appalachian woods, the leaves barely hanging on in the late afternoon light, when I've wanted only a clean topple—without creak of protest or angst. (Am I also talking here about aging?) On such days a tree creak, like that one by the river, sounds distinctly wrong, and a part of me wants to climb up, untangle high branches, and bring down the leaning tree, anything to end that incessant groaning.

A new type of musical dissonance was likewise greeted early on by consternation, ridicule, and fear. At the 1913 premiere of Stravinsky's *The Rite of Spring*, the mood of the well-dressed Parisians at the Théâtre des Champs-Élysées deteriorated from civility to surprise to dismay and then to boos and jeers as the music veered from its haunting opening into harsh dissonance. It wasn't long before agitation escalated into shouting matches about the merits of the music, while the orchestra, trying to hear themselves above the din of crowd, played louder and louder and distracted dancers lost track of the beat. Tuxedoed men climbed onto their seats and shook their fists; scuffles spilled into the aisles. Stravinsky, stunned by the reception, made a fast exit from the wings, while police were called in to quell what had become a full-blown riot—which seemed to me, that afternoon in the screeching woods, a reasonable response.

———

Years ago in a wilderness seminar, a tracking teacher taught the other participants and me about directional listening. The strategy had nothing to do with high-tech radar or the microphones spies slip under lamps on their subjects' desks. It's closer to the old trick of leaning against a wall with a glass pressed to your ear, the better to hear the murmurings on the other side. But this field technique requires only your hands, which you cup behind your ears, as you turn your head this way and that until the sound becomes clearer.

The first time I did it, cupping my hands and then dropping them, I found it was true: the world seemed to move in a little closer and then away. But when the tracker whispered, "Hear it?

Turkeys at four o'clock!" and I pivoted in that direction, hands to my ears, I heard nothing, or perhaps some faint, faraway shuffle that could easily have been someone's muffled cough. If turkeys were out there, they were to me as silent as they were invisible, yet another reminder of my aural shortcomings.

When Kassi ran off that late afternoon along the river in her usual pursuit of chipmunks, I lay down in the leaves, closed my eyes, and tried to follow with cupped hands and swiveling head that creak, which seemed to shift from one high-up place to another—above me, then back to the right. Maybe it wasn't a tree at all but a critter of some sort. But no, I'd heard it for too many months in almost the same place, and I knew enough about wildlife to know no squirrel or crow would take up the same position every time I wandered there. And it didn't chatter or caw; it creaked, stuttered, and scraped. And then I heard a rustle of leaves and panting and felt Kassi's tongue mopping every inch of my face. An old trick, I told her: disguising impatience with affection, perhaps akin to my attempt to redefine discord with careful attention, as if precise listening could change how I heard it.

Uninterested in such mental gymnastics, Kassi was already down the trail, and then so was I, and from somewhere above us the creaking went on, unlocatable and eerie. Perhaps that seeming sourcelessness, that out-of-nowhere quality, is in part why certain sounds can seem so discordant. If we name them, find the pattern in which they *do* fit, they might seem, not wrong, but merely odd. Schoenberg again: *dissonances . . . are not incomprehensible so long as they occur in the right surroundings.*

That might be musically true, but I've known people—been one myself at times—under the influence of what I might call the delusion of dissonance without a context. We mix things up, hurt and confound the people we love, create a ruckus of discord, all of which we defend by claiming that no one, alas, understands us. This is a lame excuse, unless our discordances have visionary properties, like Emily Dickinson's or Albert Einstein's, and thus assert their own value.

How, then, to tell the difference between dissonance and error, or between idiosyncrasies and brilliance?

A few propositions: Dissonance inspires patience. Discord, correction. Discord is neither arranged nor disarranged; it's haphazard, without any sense of audience or of any sound larger than itself—an ear-muffed dolphin in a closet with a drumstick attached to its flipper. Dissonance, however, is a seal wobbled by currents on its way to a fish-rich cove. It has a direction in mind. Dissonance expects to be heard. It's composed. There's a backstage plan that means some new potential—an unexpected feeling, a redefinition—has consciously entered the scene and altered the melodic line, creating a need for resolution. When two people argue, the one who recognizes the dissonance between them has more hope for resolution than does the one who hears only discord.

Back at the piano, I try pausing on that dissonant moment in Mozart's sonata, not because the tempo tells me to, but because I want to hear, really hear, what happens. Inside my ears, I've learned, those notes are setting off frequencies that interfere with each other, causing a cochlear collision of what audiologists call "critical bands." No wonder we wonder if something's amiss. On the piano I press those keys again and again, trying to see if I can separate one sound from the other, untangle what seems inharmoniously meshed, *listen* to them as the notes Mozart chose more than two hundred years ago so that we would learn to wait, senses heightened, for the resolution he's orchestrated next.

Mozart had a pet starling that supposedly influenced his revision of a piano concerto. He also had a canary, which interests me more: a clear beauty, the death of which prophesies danger in deep mines. Though Mozart called it one of the "most blameless creatures of our household," in the last hours of his life the canary agitated him so strongly that he banished it from his room. Who knows whether the fever shortened his temper, making the bird's melodic trills unbearable, or whether he thought silence a more fitting end for himself?

What we do know is that starting some two hundred years before Mozart, canaries had been captured, domesticated, and carefully bred in Germany. Birdsong had become faddish; pet owners even arranged "performances." Competitions pitted canary against canary, the birds going throat to throat for the most melodic phrase, most liquid song. It amuses me to imagine their managers prepping the birds, coaching their delivery and praising their poise, but what intrigues me is what—inevitably, I suppose—came next: based on the beauty of the song, ornithologists who catered to the fad began to decide which bird should mate with which and which shouldn't mate at all. They were bred, in other words, for the musicality of their sounds. The result? If you compare the sonograms of those domesticated canaries versus wild canaries today, you can see a distinct difference in the third and fourth seconds of their song. On the domesticated bird's sonogram, the markings on the graph (indicating frequency and duration of notes) are consistent, as if drawn by an accomplished graphic artist who'd learned to replicate the same graceful squiggle over and over again. That bird is repeating its clear notes. That bird gets cheered at competitions.

But at that same moment on the wild canary's graph, the markings go haywire, as if drawn by a kindergartener with a broken hand. Their thicknesses vary wildly; splotches hover over skew-jawed jabs. Birders studying the sonogram call this the canary's "dissonant phrase." Though it's been completely bred out of domesticated canaries, it remains distinct in wild ones, the sound harsh and jumbled.

No chance, I suppose, of it being bred out of humans. The world impinges; the soul responds or retreats. The result is often both messy and enlivening. The trick to distinguishing dissonance from mere discord is, perhaps, keeping an eye on one's wish to mythologize. Despite my old longing to see meaning everywhere, I see now that the sound of those geese overhead amounts to nothing that matters. Mere happenstance. Only banality followed: Caitlin lobbed a rock that splashed Samantha, who wailed until her mother picked her up, while out on the far end of the lake the birds resumed their cacophonous honking. And those creaking trees? Perhaps equally mundane, though sometimes just thinking about "mere" noise can lead to unexpected insights—about aging, in this case, and the sound of friction between young and old, even within one's body.

But dissonance is a different story. It has, in fact, taken me months of practicing that sonata to realize what I like most in that measure: the state of being put on alert, feeling a jolt that requires vigilance. Dissonance makes me *want* to listen to what seems wrong, to what needs something more. Within its design, in other words, is a summons to the work that lies ahead. For me, that work seems to be a kind of recomposing of my life, which now feels at times wackily out of tune, a series of unexpected notes. My writing time is squeezed between practice sessions at the piano; my garden is full of weeds; the stack of books I'd been saving for retirement is buried beneath scores and recordings of Beethoven and Bach. Or maybe all this is merely another way to delay thinking about mortality—or the necessary dissonance that can disturb any tidy conformity to plans, that can prepare us to be flexible in the face of the unknowable future.

Maybe we can't always tell the difference between dissonance that might lead to resolution and the tuneless, discordant obsession of an aging fool, in which case the words of poet Wallace Stevens matter even more: *I perceive the stick in the water as broken*, he says, *but I certainly do not try to straighten it. On the contrary, I measure the distortion.* What better way to measure this late-in-life distortion than to put myself at the feet of masters like Mozart and my teacher, who week after week reminds me that at its best a daily practice doesn't smooth the edges of dissonance; it helps me to hear the richness in it.

For now we see through a glass, darkly, the Bible claims. For me, it's more like *Now we hear through a thick wall, barely.* How much do I miss? How much cluck and chirp, woof and trill, burrow, gnash, and last breaths go on while I walk, oblivious, among it all, preoccupied with this or that, or intent on listening only for sweet melodies? The answer is "plenty," though I am hearing more these days than I used to. Maybe the biggest challenge now is to expand my notion of harmony so that it includes even the unlocatable creaks of the dying, the screeches of healthy discontents, the cacophonies of want, all the unnerving sounds that accompany so much of our jostling attempts to make sense of how we live. Leonardo da Vinci, then, would be right after all, because in the soul's composition, harmony wouldn't mean just resolution but also everything that leads us there.

What seems to be leading me these days is a wish to move, ear first, a little closer to what surrounds me, to close my eyes and hear how dissonance can agitate the spirit, widen the spectrum—be it musically, psychologically, or philosophically. I blame Mozart and my teacher for such extravagant longings. It's as if they've conspired to hoist one end of a giant glass to my ear and to press the rim against an invisible wall, to help me hear the dissonance that can both disarrange and recompose.

5

Mile 11

———————

When death, that one unstoppable syllable, ricochets in the ear, I think I have to choose between distance and detail. Climb the outcropping or wade on in? Measure or immerse?

———————

Samantha watches as her footprints in the mud fill up with water and disappear.

———————

Every day is another test of the prevailing story.

Want to deepen your nostalgia? Imagine you're a river that believes in *once upon a place*.

———————

Meanwhile, pebbles keep up their seaward scrape, which Darwin called the wild music of their destiny.

6

To Keep an Ear to the Ground

Put your ear down close to your soul and listen hard.
ANNE SEXTON

In China long ago, people hid drums inside holes they'd dug along ancient roadways. To put an ear to the ground was to bend down, miles, maybe days, later and listen for the deep percussion of the enemy's boots approaching.

In Antarctica, marine biologists, stretched out on their bellies with their heads turned sideways on the ice, heard—down there in the deep, dark cold—the ancient songs of penguins.

Sometimes when I put my ear to the ground, I make my own arbitrary rules: No listening for anything I might expect. No listening for anything that has a plan for me. No listening to anything that knows I'm listening. No pretending to listen to what bores me utterly. One day late last summer, when Samantha and I were walking along the river near Warnick's Point, we lay down in a fern-filled clearing, turned our heads sideways, and pressed our ears to the ground. Above us, the fronds waved like small green flags of allegiance to a country with no congress, to a time when listening to the soul might have meant saving your life.

More rules: No listening to blather. No not listening to her. So when she, ear to the ground, whispered, "Meemi, what are we doing?" I added another rule: No making her listen to what might be my blather. I said nothing about the soul. "Listening to the dirt," I whispered back, and she, happy as any five-year-old for a reason to lie on the ground, stopped wiggling again.

If we'd had better ears to the ground that day in the woods, we might have actually heard the unexpected: a rapid series of snaps, a soft popping, a whispered rat-a-tat. Ears cannot widen, but eyes can, and ours might have, as we turned our heads this way and that and tried to find the source of that light smattering sound. Not rain or bird droppings, not cricket wings or leaf fall. No enemy or ancient song, as the scout and the scientist have been trained to hear, though I might argue that poor listening can also, in fact, be both. How often, after all, have our own deaf ears been a cause of hostility and longing?

We lay there for a full three minutes and heard at first just the whish of ferns and, higher up, occasional bird song.

For days, my walks had been full of pinnae and rachis, the difference between lobed and toothed, and the determination to distinguish between evergreen and spinulose wood ferns. And it's not just the language that boggles. The difference between them, for example, is the relative size of the innermost lower pinnule of basal pinnae below the costa. Between the pages of my *Field Guide to Ferns* I'd stuffed fronds, sketches of fronds, and notes about rhizomes and stipes. At night for the last week I'd been lying awake, the windows open, the forest just a few steps away, and reseeing those wide swaths of green out there, which had looked for years like wide swaths of green but which had begun now to split into clumps of emerald and fir and sage gray. To spend time in the woods these past few days was to be on my knees, ticking off the distinctions—color, spore patterns, blade shape—and to know the comforts of taxonomies, of things in their proper place.

"I think this one's a bracken," a friend said, pointing, one day when we were out, calf deep in the undergrowth. To our right, the ridge rose steeply, its flanks a blurry mess of maple and oak. To our left, the trout-laden Savage River gurgled under hemlocks. But in front of us that fern usurped center stage, became the puzzle I wanted to solve. Silently, I ran down the checklist and finally announced, "Nope, brackens have blades in three parts." Sometimes things keep dividing and subdividing, not just the frond and the field guide's method of keying but my smug notions of accomplishment: knowing ferns is a higher skill, I'd decided that week, than knowing wildflowers, which is more complicated than knowing the names of mushrooms; the former, in fact, is better than the latter unless you're lost in the woods and starving. And on it went, until I had, in a few seconds of taxonomic nitpicking, removed myself from that walk, my friend, that lush ferny valley into which I love to disappear. I know, I know: God's in the details. But so's the devil, and that day—maybe increasingly every day—what I want more than heaven or hell is this resounding earth.

⸻

Two hours away the Phipps Conservatory in Pittsburgh devotes a whole room to ferns. They spill into the damp walkway, tower overhead, rise in clumps and spread in swaths, some new, some ragged. After the next-door Orchid Room with its splashes of color and audible human gasps of delight, people move through the Fern Room quietly, barely stopping. In the hour I sat and stood and strolled there one day, the only conversation took place between two men obviously waiting for others in their party still lingering among the orchids. "Investments," I overhead. And "digital," "three years," and "fast turnaround." Talk, I assumed, about doing something now which might pay off in the future. Meanwhile, nothing in this room would attract birds or bees or butterflies or any other means of reproduction. When it comes to building for the future, ferns are on their own. To scatter their spore, they need only a bit of moisture, the slightest breeze.

To see the largest ferns—Tasmanian Tree Ferns, the label said—I, who'd left my field guide at home this time, had to crane my neck. Its rhizome, instead of lying horizontal on or under the ground, rose from its hairy base straight up almost to the ceiling, where it flared into a canopy of fronds close to fifteen feet across. *This is the forest primeval*, Longfellow intoned. *Bearded with moss, and in garments green, indistinct in the twilight*, but I, standing under the tallest ones, thought of a time more primeval than even that of *Evangeline*, a languorous time, 350 million years ago, before birds and blossoms, when nothing strode and overhead was only the swish of fronds the size of small trees and the wing hum of giant dragonflies, a time when hundred-foot-high club mosses creaked in overhead breezes. To keep an ear to the ground in that ancient world would have meant long, slow times of silence, broken only by the occasional slurp of mud under the feet of giant centipedes and, from the earliest ferns, periodic spurts of spores so large their plunk to the ground might have been cause for alarm.

Had we humans, still 349 million years off in the future, been there, we might have noted the quiet intimacy with rain, its invitations to hunker down, the huddles of green, damp feet, and dark corners, the kind of place, Loren Eiseley says, in which you strain to hear *the undernote of long-dead activity, of something that lingered, that would linger till the last stone had fallen, something that would not go away.*

Isn't this, finally, what the soul—whatever it is—wants: neither the past nor the future (it isn't interested in time) but the attentive ear of the one whose life it makes restless? It doesn't want story; it wants to hear itself.

As I surreptitiously flipped a fern pinnule over to look for spores, a young woman entered the room, sat down quietly on a mossy stone bench, unbuttoned her blouse, and lifted her baby to bared breast. A giant frond arched over and in front of them so that from where I stood, the baby's head, bald, and the breast, pale, almost shone from behind a feathery veil, both of them half-hidden by the drooping, dripping green mantle of too much musing. The blouse draped open, the baby's mouth widened, and as the woman leaned her head back against the bench, her face went slack. Memorize this, I told myself, this palimpsest, this momentary juxtaposing of tattered and fresh, this adjacency of images that might mean the kind of resonance I long for is occasionally possible.

Picture yourself in Samantha's position: your own head on the ground, ear in the dirt. Shift your eyes up to the arching frond swaying above your forehead. See the collection of darker dots speckling the pinnule's undersides? When conditions are right—when the pressures of adhesion and cohesion inside each cell destabilize, causing the annulus to arch backward, stretching and finally splitting the front of the capsule, and a lot of other things happen that I don't understand—the annuluses all start snapping like a legion of catapults. We're not talking about Roman warlords launching boulders down a hill into the enemy's path; we're talking about thousands of almost invisible capsules ripping open and flinging millions of invisible spores, and each of them doing so with a sharp snap that our too-insensitive human ears cannot hear. Special equipment, though, can; the sound has been described as akin to popcorn popping or a series of quick metallic clicks, the rapid detonation of tiny explosives. *Dehiscence*, the process is called, from *dehiscere*: to gape open.

Perhaps that's what the soul wants to hear: not the sounds of recounting, not *next, next, next,* but the sounds of openings—*unwrap, widen.* If in those rare moments something bares itself, even gleams, let us take note. Or as Eiseley might say, let us take undernote. At such moments, *to put the ear to* might involve not just ground but the ground below ground. Layers of sound, and the accompanying risk, which composer John Cage knew so well: *No one*, he said, *can have* an *idea once he starts really listening.*

Just above my head that day under the ferns with Samantha, dehiscence—I like the word—was likely underway: tiny capsules snapping open, sprinkling the ground around us, perhaps even our hair, with the possibility of next generations. Such moments are but moments—ephemeral, maybe inconsequential—but they can shift the tone of the hour, resonate through the rest of the day. What would happen, for instance, if we knew that whole layers of the world—underfoot, overhead, and everywhere in between—had their own sonic realms? How would we spend our years? How might we develop our ears?

Maybe these are just the mutterings of a woman who on a particular day was tired of distinctions, the precision of logic. Maybe she feels her life has passed another turning point, the mumbly price one pays for wrapping one's hands around the worn wooden wheel of an old clipper ship and leaning into it, hard, to begin the final turn. To turn a big ship, like a long life, takes some doing, but I'm telling you that that day among the ferns I felt the first creaks of a final turn, and what buoyed me was not the sharpness of a nimble mind, deducing, identifying, concluding. It wasn't reason, in other words, the rational linking of idea A to idea B. It was resonance, the languorous mind sidling up to, sympathetic with, those layered images of pale gleam among the heavy green, the hearkening ear reverberating with what surrounds it. Immersion, entanglement, vibrancy.

Maybe I did try to do what Anne Sexton says we should: *put your ear down close to your soul and listen hard.* But whatever the soul might have said, I missed it. Instead, Samantha and I lay still on the ground that afternoon among the ferns, listening to stinkbugs and chipmunks on the dry forest floor and a crow high overhead until she whispered to me, "Meemi, do you remember me back then when I was old?" I rolled my head toward her, knowing it wasn't the malarkey of past lives and some form of reincarnation that I heard but a time when the imagination had its anchor in the ancient mud, before we came to believe our everyday lives constituted a series of crises, a state of alarm that means the anchors, too shallowly set, have begun to drag again.

Whatever she meant by that odd comment (she's five years old!), I wanted to put my head—my ear, in fact—to her copper curls. "Yes," I wanted to be able to say to her, "yes, I do."

But of course I don't. Nor was I sure what to say next—something about the arc of one's life or the ever larger histories of where we have landed, where we find ourselves? Something about ferns as indirect descendants, about continental collisions, the dust of extinctions, the fact that the club moss down the path, for instance, once towered a hundred feet overhead and that ferns are not the only thing that's withered? What, Loren Eiseley, would you have said at such a moment about undernotes and things that linger?

"Look," I said instead, reaching up to turn a fern pinna over. "See the spores?" She ran her finger over the bumps. "They'll shoot out into the air. People used to believe if you caught one, you became invisible."

"Let's try," she whispered.

"You have to listen hard for the popping first," I told her, "and be ready to catch them." She repositioned her ear to the ground and cupped her hands.

I did not have to ask her why she might wish to be invisible. Aren't most kids ready to relax their sense of self, become an imp with an ear for trouble or fun?

The release and soft landings—of spores and who knows what else—are beyond the hearing of a naked human ear, but that isn't the point. Growth, after all, is notoriously less audible than ruin. No, the point is this: We oscillate between reason and resonance, and on those days among the ferns it was resonance—the pitch of the day, the tenor of those images: bald baby, bare breast, Samantha's pale face among the profusion of greens—that lingered. The arc of time piled up in the present, setting even the past to vibrating, reminding me that a German romantic once posited the existence of the "ear-soul." Surreal, for sure, but picture it there, at the far end of a dark canal: the delicate bones, the thin membrane, and the fluid, always the fluid, upon which our balance depends.

7

Mile 13

NEAR WARNICK'S POINT

———

Sorting stones beside the river, Samantha says, "Some nights I'm a door."

———

Can anything, including us, that takes pride in its current shape reenter the past? Or be wise about the future?

———

Erosion: the river gurgles fast around the outside curve of a muddy bank, pries loose the embedded twigs. Year after year, ripple, scrape, and slump—the sounds of the Savage changing the shape of its valley.

8

A True Seer *Hears*

Most of the ninety thousand species of insects on this planet use sound to court and to warn. The horned passalus, a kind of beetle, rubs one of its legs against a textured part of its own abdomen. Picture your torso as a washboard you can strum with your knees so adroitly that you end up not with cramping back muscles or whatever other damage such contortions might cause but with the music of seventeen different sounds floating through the evening air. Or under the water. That's the setting for an arthropod the size of a paper clip whose mating call rivals the decibel level of motorcycles. Water must muffle the female's sound receptors. Or maybe she forgives the noise of his antics for the chance to mate with a bug whose gestures she can't resist. How many females, after all, wouldn't sidle up to a male floating across the pond with his right paramere's *pars stridens*—something like a penis with a hand— stroking his own abdomen?

Insects outnumber humans by two hundred million to one. Most of them hear, most of them make noise—clicking grasshoppers, stridulating dung beetles, head-banging termites, fruit flies who flirt by waving one wing, crickets who rub their legs together and unsilence the night. They reproduce prodigiously, millions of them cranking out two or three, up to twenty-five, generations a year, and except for the usual crickets and cicadas, most of them do it out of audible reach of the likes of me, who rose early this morning to sit on a downed hemlock between river and field and test the truth of a poem I loved many years ago. *You will never be alone*, William Stafford wrote, *you hear so deep / a sound when autumn comes*. Though autumn has not quite come to Appalachia, I still hear in his lines that suggestion of universal coherence for which I've often longed. Except for a woolly bear caterpillar inching across the log by my leg, I seem to be by myself in this predawn darkness. I'm listening. Overhead the stars are silent. Across the valley nothing moves. Except for the river's quiet ripple, I don't hear a thing.

In the fable that opens Rachel Carson's *Silent Spring*, what's been silenced are songbirds, poultry flocks, honeybees, fruit, fish, voices—human and otherwise. Vitality, in other words, has been leached from the land. The fable warns about the dangers of pesticides, a warning so well heeded for a while that it launched the modern environmental movement. As a little girl traipsing through the woods around her Pennsylvania home, Carson had not only seen but listened to a world full of the sounds of small creatures, listened so carefully she knew herself as part of that world, a sneezing, breathing, sighing, humming human being, a body, even when languageless, alive among the small splashes of river pools and fox yips in wooded hills. When those sounds were poisoned to silence, she heard that too. Dying of breast cancer while the pesticide industry unleashed a well-financed and vicious assault against her, Carson wrote this near the end of her life: *I never hear these [bird] calls without a wave of . . . many emotions—a sense of lonely distances, a compassionate awareness of small lives controlled by forces beyond volition or denial, a surging wonder at the sure instinct for route and direction that so far has baffled human efforts to explain it.*

Nose deep in insect books for the past few weeks, I've been reading about bugs' ears. The woolly bear caterpillar next to me on the log, for instance, has none. No amount of my shouting or singing or reciting poems would make it turn its charred-looking head. But if I stood up and stomped on this log we're sharing, the hundreds of brown and copper hairs—setae—on its bristly body would act like tuning forks. Set in motion by the sound waves exploding from my foot, the ruffling tufts would translate as danger. The woolly bear would curl into a tight ball, wait out the storm like a furry nugget of amber.

Peril averted, it will spend this part of its life crawling silently over the ground, munching what it can, surviving the winter coiled under bark or log or rock. There, its heart will stop beating. As temperatures drop, its guts will freeze, then its blood, then the rest of its body. Its tissues soaked with a cryoprotectant, the frigid body will know nothing of cold snaps or January thaws, the blizzard we're likely to get in March. It will weather the winter in icy motionlessness.

Read almost any of the major creation myths—Judaic, Christian, Islamic, Maori—and see what precedes the beginning: cold, dark voids; motionless calm; black, boundless vacancy; interminable stillness; perhaps what this woolly bear will feel in a few months. See, too, that Genesis, for example, means rupturing that stillness with the Word. From there it's a free-for-all of noisy creation: ripened fruit drops, wings flap, beasts multiply. The whole shebang unleashed, the world becomes a place of niches and noise, teeming profligacy and a million tongues, the origin of both blather and song. From then on, sustained silences—personal, ecological, political—have worried some of us: do they precede some kind of creative explosion or do they signal yet another kind of death?

They do neither, of course, for those who haven't listened. There is, in fact, no such thing as silence—ominous or rewarding—to those who've never heard the sounds that surround them. Rachel Carson not only taught us to pay attention but to distinguish between blather and song, and between the quiet of mornings like this one and that other quiet, which means something vital has vanished. The quality of her listening has also helped train me to hear both large and small losses. Remembering the Lettermen can turn me, a middle-aged woman, into a teeny bopper at a make-out party in George Toder's basement. Some Saturday mornings, listening for the routine phone call my mother will never make to me again, I'm forty, thirty-five, twenty-two, in need of her advice, even if I'm not.

Because of Rachel Carson, I think I'm learning how to listen stereophonically. At a certain point in one's life, the mind isn't really a blank slate; it has its positions and predispositions. But she has taught me to ready myself, to anticipate, somewhat unfocused, turning this way and that. Grateful for ears on both sides of the head, I try to collect what's out here by listening for what isn't.

If Carson had not sounded the alarm fifty years ago, the silence of this early dawn might be disturbing. I might be thinking about Stafford's poem while overhead the crushed confetti of DDT-thinned eggshells litters the nests and underfoot earthworms move the poisoned dirt in and out of their bodies, make themselves plump targets for doomed robins, while nearby a barred owl (I've heard it hundreds of times: *who cooks for you? who cooks for you?*) twitches on the forest floor. The fields and woods might be as she described: blighted, silent, withered, and fruitless, without birdsong, chipmunk chatter, cricket calls. My listening would be full of worry and lament.

Instead, these mountains are, for now, reasonably robust. There's a moratorium on fracking in Maryland, and plenty of volunteers patrol the river for signs of pollution. There's time, at least for a while, to listen for what's underfoot at this moment, what's in the air, for any of the lip-smacking, tongue-hissing, panted-breath sounds of evolution and adaptation that have landed me here, watching this earless woolly bear go about its daily rounds in the early dawn while overhead a bat swoops among treetops.

Seventy to eighty percent of the creatures alive out here are insects. Though most of them stake their ability to eat, survive, and mate on their ability to hear, none of them have ears like ours—sound-trapping projections on both sides of the head. In fact, so separately have we developed from them, their ears—evolutionarily speaking—are not even related to ours. Remember the tuning fork setae of this woolly bear that are not vibrating at the moment because I'm not stomping my foot? They are its "ears." Hinged at their base to the caterpillar's cuticle, they respond to sound waves, especially from the rear, especially as a bat, sonar blipping, closes in with open mouth.

Other insects sport their hearing organs wherever they can— on the tips of their antennae, inside their mouths, on their knee caps or chests, behind their heads. Those "ears" take the forms of sound-sensitive drums made of levers and pistons, sensitive membranes and tiny cavities of air. The fruit fly has a feathery wand; the cockroach, a set of bristles. The male mosquito, a complicated system of levers and shafts on his head. If he's awake now in this predawn light, he's likely listening for the low-frequency sounds a female emits via wing beat. When his tiny hairs begin to quiver— that is, when he hears her with his body—he'll lift his wings and fly toward her, the vibrations on his head triggering him to seize her and clasp.

By my side, the woolly bear caterpillar has turned north on the log and begun to inch toward my thumb. If it survives the winter and spins its pupae next spring, it will emerge as a moth with newly grown tympanic membranes on either side of its head, which is not much bigger than a big grain of sand. Then the moth and the bat now circling overhead will listen hard for one another. If the moth, flitting from tree to tree, detects the oncoming echolocating cries of its number-one predator, it will, in midair, activate its tymbal, the drum-like structure stretched over a small cavity on its chest, emitting its own rhythmic pulse. The bat, aiming for a direct hit, will be thrown off course. Unable to find its prey in the dark, it will continue its high-pitched cries, flying erratically in search of the moth, which, also flying erratically, will continue to pulse its tymbals—jamming the bat's radar—until the bat gives up and heads elsewhere. The moth, of course, isn't thinking about jamming frequencies or ultrasonic clicks. In fact, so reflexive is its defensive pulsing that its body will continue to emit the pulse for a good three hours after that tiny head has been severed in a lab.

Scientists love this stuff. So do I. Imagine devoting your life to listening to what can't easily be heard. Researchers have, in fact, filled millions of pages and thousands of websites with studies of every part of insect body structures and functions, including auditory. They've dribbled water on insect "ears," dolloped them with shellac and flour, smeared them with Vaseline, corralled bugs in boxes with recordings of crows, plucked the hairs off their backs, serenaded their lab cages, barraged them with low-frequency tones. Trying to discover hearing thresholds, impairments, purposes, they arm themselves with tiny weight scales, electron microscopes, and sophisticated amplifiers, recording the hisses of Madagascar cockroaches and the squeaks of death's-head hawkmoths.

Sitting here on this summer morning, waiting for the sun, I, of course, can hear no such commotion. Which is, in many ways, a blessing. Who could bear that kind of cacophony? But to ignore what we cannot hear may be worse. It's what Carson railed against: the silence that's born of hubris.

I see now I must listen not so much with lament or anticipation but with a better sense of limitations. Though I close my eyes and concentrate, the tympanic membranes inside my immovable, flat-against-my-head ears aren't dainty enough to pick up the zillions of sound waves I know are at this very moment pulsing across the field, through the trees, along this log where the woolly bear has turned again and headed away from my thumb. I sit here, as if deaf, as if I've been booted from the world of hearing, backed into a soundproof room in which the only noise comes from me—the scrape of my pants on the bark and the occasional sniffle from my nose.

Carson's job was to anticipate the silence that could follow damage—to eggs in nests, reproductive capabilities, liver functions, small lungs, nervous systems, and children's brains. She was a seer who, armed with careful research, heard her way into the future. When she published *Silent Spring*, many dismissed it as the work of a hysterical woman. Unable—or unwilling—to distinguish between the scientific basis of her passion and the outcries of apocalyptic kooks who claim the world will end next week, critics—many of them allied with chemical industries—carped for decades. Some continue even today. The silent spring she warned about was averted only because wiser minds prevailed, minds informed by the accuracy of her work.

Can we simultaneously hear what's not yet come, what's here, and what's gone? Polyphonic silences, like polyphonic music, demand deep listening. Such listeners historically have been called seers, or fools—the difference is sometimes very slight. Is a fool someone whose listening has not yet led to truths? Or someone who hears sounds that do not exist and never have existed, nor ever will? And can one hear too much? Perhaps to truly hear the world requires both heightened sensitivity and a fair amount of filtering and skepticism. Balance, in other words.

Given the physical limits of my paltry hearing, the least I can do is to make a stab at knowing what I don't know, to risk being a fool, to sit here in this early morning silence and realize that across the river and up in the woods, even here on this log, hundreds of small creatures are vibrating their vocal chords, smashing their wings, strumming their abdomens, filling their lungs with presong, drumming their tymbals, all their zillions of attempts to survive, to eat, to mate—and I can hear none of it. Meanwhile, the woolly bear has silently rounded the log, begun to descend the opposite side.

Perhaps what Stafford means after all is not that we can literally *hear so deep / a sound when autumn comes* but that if we can imagine or imagine remembering that sound—*all* those sounds—maybe then *the whole wide world pours down*. Or at least the whole wide world might inch a little closer, click by strum by belly-scraping song. And if it doesn't, maybe then we'll know, as Rachel Carson certainly did, which silences prevent that pouring down, which ones, in other words, mean we could be increasingly alone.

9

Listening to the Same River Twice

THEME AND VARIATIONS

You cannot step in the same river twice.

HERACLITES

Like so much in the natural world—aspens in the wind, wood thrush songs, and peepers' calls—a river, from a certain distance, can sound soothing. It's full of repeated trills and steady rhythms, soft spurtles, a background reminder of quiet continuity, the appealing murmur of things in their place.

Rippling along this sunny summer afternoon, the Savage flows familiarly through the valley in eastern Garrett County, headed south toward the Potomac River, which will eventually wander, slow and deep—maybe even soothingly—through the nation's capital. Up here in the mountains, though, it's rocky, brisk but wadable. After pulling on rubber boots, I step off the bank and make my way out into the streambed, to the confluence of the Savage and a tributary known locally as Poplar Lick.

Last night, restless again, I'd resorted to a CD I'd borrowed weeks ago from a friend. She has a whole collection of sleep-inducing discs: Hindu chants, the sounds of oceans and rain and running water. The running water one has been collecting dust in my night-table drawer. The sound soothes her, she says, drowns out the buzz of midnight angst, lulls her back to sleep. At 3:00 a.m., I tried it, turning the volume low and listening, wide eyed, to the ceaseless sound of chafe and clash.

Perhaps I know too much—that rivers are in the business of eating up stone and undermining banks. They work like rasps against a lip of dolomite or granite, grinding and gouging. They can lug tons of topsoil, ferry logs, chisel three feet a year off the edge of a cliff, dramatically change the landscape.

Perhaps my friend can just let the sound of a river's uninterrupted flow—its quiet undercurrent—quiet her mind, while I, restless, have been doomed to think too much about the river's frictions and the enigmas they suggest about character, conflict, and the vexing sense I have of the self as a fluid form in need of shaping.

But today, water swirling now around my calves, I'm frazzled and aiming to listen to the river as she does. I've been reading Barry Lopez—*the sound of fish dreaming, twilight in a still pool downstream*— even William Congreve: *Music has charms to soothe the savage breast, / To soften rocks*. A part of me wants to see if it's possible to forget what I know and to hear the way a river might erase a few angsts.

———

Erasing boundary angsts was what Maryland's governor had in mind in 1872 when he proclaimed that the eastern boundary of Garrett County shall run from the spot where the Mason-Dixon Line crosses the ridge of Savage Mountain straight southwest to the mouth of the Savage River, where it dumps into the Potomac. The problem is that rivers and their mouths—like us—don't always lie still in their beds. The Savage can flood and ebb, its endpoint churn a little to the west and then to the east. Given the possibility of wandering mouths, it's impossible to know exactly where the river ends.

And given the unlikelihood of a "true self" as some inviolable thing that must be brought to the surface and allowed to shine, it's even harder to know how to imagine ourselves. Standing in the river, I know I'm pushing this analogy, but what would happen if we imagined ourselves as unfixed meanderers roving within a channel, responding to the sounds of our locales and the smells of our own geology?

States can't tolerate the ambiguous boundaries we humans often live with. This is especially true if a river serves as boundary between two entities (think Iraq and Iran, Maryland and Virginia). In such cases, an exact and stable centerline of the river needs to be pinpointed, a line that remains essentially unchanged by conditions on the surface. Politicians call that the border.

Hydrologists call it the thalweg: the "valley way," the deepest continuous inline in a river, the lowest invisible current, the flow of slightest friction, the deep-sunk line of least resistance.

When I told her this, my friend nodded. "Yes," she said, "that's it. That's what I want to listen to."

—⁓—

The Savage is technically a first-order, perennial, high-gradient, headwater stream with boulder-cobble bedrock. Here at this confluence, it looks like a river just poured from a blender, still frothy. The splash and spray mean lots of churned-in oxygen, which means lots of trout, which often means a lot of anglers, none of whom are here today, which means I can obsess without interruption about sound and balm and the nature of the self. All that.

A few miles south of here, just above the dam, you can wade in the seemingly still water of the reservoir and listen to a raucous caw overhead, a light step in the forest, the plop of fish or frog, water lapping against your ankles. But from where I'm standing this summer day wearing galoshes and hat, the hills rise steeply from the Savage River's narrow valley. The water—clear and cold—plunges and rolls, produces an almost constant hum.

If I were at the piano, I'd be thinking *intervals of thirds in three-quarter time descending the whole length of the keyboard*. Any sound from the surrounding hills—so thick with slicks of rhododendron you'd need a machete to scramble through—is drowned by the river. It's useless, in other words, to stand here and try to listen to anything but water.

If my friend were nearby and I wanted to say, "Let's get out of here," I'd likely have to motion with my arm. Over the river's racket, words wouldn't reach her, nor would that thalweg she wants to fall asleep to. Maybe only when it's quiet is there a chance that other river might rise more audibly to the surface. Our job, then, would be to learn what to do with it.

But what's the difference, I'd want to ask her, between being mesmerized by insistent, wordless sound versus being dulled by the same? Does one have to do with giving yourself over to it, the other with giving in?

———

When my piano teacher plays one of Schubert's impromptus and I can listen without envy to those falling arpeggios, I hear how one note creates the need for the next, approaches some edge, pauses for a beat, tilts, and then plummets in a cascade of sound, not buoyant but inevitable, over the invisible cliff in what can only be called release, resonance.

"Think," she says, dropping her hands into her lap, "of weight being passed from one finger to the next. Imagine you're handing off a burden."

I suspect my friend would say *that* is what she needs in the middle of the night.

But what to hand off? What to hold on to? How do we know what we need in order to become who we are? Work. Is it work?

———

The thalweg, of course, has no literal reality. Even if you drained the whole river and hiked the rocky bottom from headwaters to mouth, it would never be visible or audible. It's an abstract concept, conceived by a fluvial geomorphologist who's hired to plot the lowest elevations in the river's channel and connect the dots. Without the mind that imagines it, it doesn't exist.

Sometimes we figure out what we need and imagine it into existence. My friend can dream up a thalweg and sleep easily till dawn. I can turn thalweg into metaphor and pretend I hear it rewatering an inner life. Perhaps we even dream up the self we listen to most.

Maybe that's what Glenn Gould meant when he said it's the *inner ear of the imagination* that can hear the *structure that suggested a way of life.*

But think of the danger of imagining voices and carrying out their directives, or of hearing a signal where there is only noise—a mistake statisticians call overfitting. What happens, I might ask my friend, if our need for a shapely life or a good night's rest means we overfit the world with our notion of how it works: creationism, constellations, perhaps even thalwegs?

———

"Legato, legato!" my teacher insists, hovering over me, turning the pages. "Listen. You must connect those notes." Hard enough in music, harder yet in the physical world, where the risk is higher. It's one thing, I tell myself, to staccato through what should be legato; it's quite another to overfit the world—or ourselves—with false connections.

———

Or to underfit: to ignore the ones that do exist.

———

Just upstream from where I'm failing to blur river sounds into lullabies, the Savage courses around a bend. On the outside edge, the water gouges and grinds, carries bits of stone away. On the inside edge, the water slows, laps against the fern-laden bank, lowers its load of soil bits and leaf debris. One side of the river scours; the other side deposits. Over here, it thunders; over there, it sloshes. Over time, the river itself will meander accordingly and so, eventually, will the thalweg, snaking from side to side, belying any government's stake in its stability. That means that just south of here, where the Savage empties into the Potomac, the mouth has likely shifted over the years, the official boundary line sliding back and forth between banks. Meandering thalweg, geologists call it.

―――

How to translate that into human terms—that undercurrent's response to the impinging world? Giving up or growing up? The self on its way to becoming yet another self? Or should I just be fascinated by, maybe envious of, the way the physical world continually adapts and reinvents itself?

―――

Water's one constant power—about which it is helpless—is to go down. But the equally mindless earth obstructs, slows the water's movement with limestone outcroppings, thick clay deposits, even the tangled root systems of riverside hemlocks. Upstream in the river's next bend, a fallen, half-submerged tree has snagged small clutches of debris. Pockets of rot and decay have begun to stall the current and create a small pool, a haven in which a host of creatures congregate: water striders and crustaceans, salamanders and worms. They cling to the stripped woody stems, a feather, ribbons of grass. Or they inch over the wet oak leaves, make forays into fast-moving water from tiny planks of half-drowned twigs, retreat to what might sound to them like a small clog of stillness around which the water tumbles.

―――

When he was two or three, Pablo Casals used to crawl under the piano while his father played. Above him the keys lifted and lowered the hammers on strings. Beneath that dark ceiling of sound, the boy, crouching or sitting, leaned his head hard against the instrument. This was no cushioned pillow; the boy, in fact, must have been uncomfortable, scrunched underneath, ear pressed tight against the wood that vibrated with every keystroke. He must have wanted the immediacy of absorption, music entering the ear without the muffling buffer of air and other sounds.

―――

Me too, which is why I'm tempted to drop to my knees on two flat stones near the river's middle, lean over, and turn and lower my head, though I know I wouldn't be anything but disappointed. The cold water would rise, glide under my neck, swirl around my right ear. At best, the result might be a chilly moment of stereophonic listening: underwater silence with one ear, the river's ripples with the other. A noble goal; a nutty attempt. Hearing two rivers at once is not, I'm sure, a matter of positioning one's head but of trying to hear two truths at once—almost impossible except in extremities: *The weight of the silence / is clearest*, poet Katherine Larson says, *when you play / Bach*.

———

The river's a crash-and-splash hodgepodge of shattered tree limbs, abandoned nests, someone's untethered fishing line. When the water's up, as it is today, it sprays and froths, climbs its bank, becomes a running discourse on flood and muck, carry and drown. If I'm listening to anything here, it's the effort to readjust my sense of scale. This river—can I even say *this* river, as if it's the same river?— has been running here for thousands of years, through changing climates and eroding mountains, wolf and elk migrations, human incursions, widespread logging, and a series of civil wars. When I step into it, I feel the puniness of human skin, the thinness of boots on stony bottom beneath this water I cannot hold or shape or stop or start. Is that what soothes my friend: the sound—in the grand scheme of things—of her own unimportance? Dipping my hands in, I listen how the river gurgles as it divides around my wrists and resumes as if I were not here, as if I were never here.

But I *have* been here many times, where Poplar Lick dumps into the Savage, here, where one time, winter camping with a now-gone lover, we nestled a few dozen candles in deep snow and lit them all at midnight; here, where I once—for reasons I no longer know—sat for an hour on a midriver rock; where one day the Savage River became the River Styx and a new series of choices began, along with the burdens they carry.

Or was that a different *I* who was *here*? Is that what Heraclites really meant? That we, fluid beings that we are, might be as likely as the river to change, become a different person stepping into a different river at the exact same place?

———

You think the world is stable? Look at its reflection in water. That hemlock on the bank—soft needled and motionless—is, in the river, a jittery finger of green blur. The images fragment, sway.

———

By late afternoon, the river has, in my mind, become a raucous cortege of hidden dramas. Rubbly bedrock here means a maze of underwater interstices, submerged and connected hallways and cubbyholes among boulders and cobbles where adult stoneflies might spend their short lives dining on their own kin's larvae while crayfish feast on carrion. The river itself was named for a man who wasn't eaten: one John Savage, whose 1736 surveying party, camped near the confluence of the Potomac and this as-yet-unnamed tributary, ran out of resources and, desperate, selected their weakest one for dinner. Luckily, supplies arrived in time; the party nixed the plan, named the river after Savage, and finished its mission a few weeks later. No word on whether Mr. Savage bolted or continued obligingly on. Infanticide, cadaver snitching, barely averted cannibalism. All that.

———

There are at least two rivers in every river. One is a stream of friction and flux; the other moves belly-flat in its bed. A third? Perhaps, though I've yet to imagine it. The first one gurgles and thrums; the second one barely shushes. To put your ear to the river is to hear the former: the *glorb* and guggle of water across a bed of gravel; the softer slurps; the dark, rooty, salamander-filled, moss-fuzzed notes and occasional clomp of hoof splashing off the edges of small, slick stones. And then the barely audible spatter every time the breeze cranks up and hemlock needles—killed off by wooly adelgids—drop from the tree to litter the water.

To hear the other, you must know something else about a river: unencumbered by friction with edges, its deep center—its thalweg—travels fast. But above it, on the surface, in the clear middle, you can watch small waves lift and lower the scalloped ripples that, no matter how quickly the current's running, don't travel with it. Catching the light a little differently, they stay in one place and quiver.

—————

"Hear this G?" my teacher asks. I'm at the piano, Beethoven's *Six Variations on a Theme* in front of me, learning to hear the way the composer wants that G note in *Variation IV* sustained with the thumb while the other fingers dance around D, C, B-flat, A. How to keep that one finger still while the others flit, lift off, land lightly again? "Hold it," Betty says, reaching over and pressing my thumb to the key with two of her own long fingers.

Hold it, I tell myself, as if it were an anchor, as if without it, I, too, might be nothing but another shapeless victim—or agent?—of erosion.

"Now listen," she says, playing those few measures. "It's as if you've been on one path and then a single note enters and part of you keeps going and the other stays right there, right on that G. Press firmly. You have to listen to both."

—————

By later afternoon the sun has dipped behind the western ridges, and the river has gone from racket to churning gurgle. Hardly the mesmerist I'd hoped to hear, though there's this consoling thought: A river can't lead you to nowhere. It might take days or weeks, but if you're lost in this country and can follow the current, you'll end up eventually in one of two oceans or a gulf.

—————

From a distance, Bette Midler sings, *there is harmony and it echoes through the land*. Yes, I might try to agree—from a distance. Serenity's a temporary illusion, though I'll take it now and then, especially on a restless night. But there's no undoing what we know; there's only hearing what we know within larger and larger contexts. The trick, it seems to me, is to not forsake the details of the music *and* the mayhem—*Hold it*, Betty might say—even if the vista widens.

―――――

What shapes us is not always pretty, and so we listen or we don't. Casals did, obsessively and alone. And whatever that deep listening was to—those delitescent, lurking undercurrents (that thalweg?)— he must have known to guard it. When he discovered Bach's long-lost *Six Suites for Violoncello Solo*, he felt intuitively that the music would shape his life. He practiced them over and over, until every turn, every sudden cascade and chord, felt like home. It took him twelve years, and in all that time, he practiced them in seclusion. It was the only way, he claimed, that he could listen to what was shaping him.

―――――

From source to mouth, a river—thalweg and rapids and slow, sloshy edges—cannot grow smaller. Whether it drowns and destroys, or gathers and joins, the river's only job is to increase and move. The word itself is a distant relative of *to arrive*, which once meant *to come to shore*.

And finally I do, climbing up on the damp, twilit bank to pull off my boots. We, of course, can—through bad choices or circumstances—grow smaller, which is why the image of a thalweg might sometimes soothe. But whether we think of ourselves as unformed or developed, one of our jobs is to parse and weigh and to live with the resulting contradictions. Listening here means listening, too, to the river within the river, meaning the river in the mind, which ripples livelier inside a paradox:

Is there a meaning to music? someone asked Aaron Copland.

Yes.

Can you state . . . what the meaning is?

No.

Hear how the river might become two rivers and then one again? Likewise, the self. Increasingly, that's the kind of lullaby I can wake up to.

10

Keys

One need not mention how often writers have employed surrogate figures to imagine the private lives of their own fathers. Literature abounds with them. In my case, I've needed two specific men: one dead fifty years before my father was born, the other gone long before I knew that I even needed him. Both of them were involved with pianos, though my father had no interest in music. There were other things—depression, despair, regret—that he seemed to have no interest in either, though I, who grew up oddly lonely under the roof he so cheerfully provided, did. When he died a few years ago and I opened the box of letters he'd written from Stalag Luft III, I missed with a pang not just the good-natured and practical man I'd known for fifty some years but the man I hadn't known either, whose nonpresence was even more palpable in those typewritten sheaves of onionskin paper he'd sent from behind barbed wire for almost two years in the mid-1940s. Was my father never, even mildly, depressed? Unsure? Unhappy—as most of us have at least momentarily been—with life?

Against the backdrop of Birkenau and Auschwitz, I know what a luxury it is to bemoan, even mildly, what internment might have done to my father. And regardless, I'm not one to whine about what hasn't happened; I find longings, in fact, to be good company and barely care that their way of luring me into good books, Bach, or long walks in the woods might look to others like self-indulgence or escape. I'm especially happy when an old yearning draws me some-place new, as the father longing did, leading me into the work of the French composer Olivier Messiaen and the enigma of a Connecticut factory owner named George Read, both of whom helped me to question the silences in my father's private life. Psychologists tell us we cannot recover what we never had, but stories and certain music, I came to find, were able to return to me—as they do to millions of others—what I didn't quite know I'd been missing. Such a return, of course, doesn't come without complications: that which restores emotionally, after all, can also sharpen the urge to unsilence the facts of the past.

———

I first heard Messiaen's *Quartet for the End of Time* five years after I read my father's POW letters. The father missing they'd stirred again had quieted. It was summer here in the Appalachians, and on a whim I had driven the seven miles from my home to an unlikely concert hall attached to a small gift shop featuring mostly Amish and Mennonite crafts, homemade jellies, and crocheted baby blankets. The building nestles in a valley not far from the farm where I buy bedding plants from women in long dresses and black bonnets and where all the plows are horse drawn. I'd never heard of Messiaen.

The Great Hall at Penn Alps is simple: no stage or velvet curtains, no lighting technician in the box behind us. Three walls of large windows destroy the usual insular effect of a good concert hall. Outside, as we listened to the concert, crows perched against the sunset on a branch of a large spruce tree. Inside, the folding chairs for the forty of us who attended were comfortable enough for an hour; they ringed the musicians' chairs and a black-lacquered grand piano that brought back memories of my own hands on an old player piano we had in our home: that cool touch of the ivory, the way the fingers could both glide and press, as from that warping upright box a sound—hesitant, out of tune—emerged that could make the room vanish into a world of trills and glissades or the sweet melancholy of a Liszt. Feeling at Penn Alps the intimacy of someone's large living room, I looked around for anyone I knew and noticed a couple of folks from a Unitarian church twenty miles away and a local patron of the arts; the rest were a mix of blue-jean-clad and long summer skirt people and two who looked as if they'd just stepped off the nearby hiking trails. The room, overlooking the Casselman River, is small. Stretching out my legs, I could easily have tripped the violinist as she walked the twenty feet from the back to the front.

But the mention of Stalag VIII in the program notes replaced the concert hall and childhood musings with the stale odor and brittle feel of my father's letters. Among them is a drawing he'd done of the camp: numbered barracks, the cookhouse and fire pools, the latrines and guardhouses. I could almost see his firm blue-penciled lines again, feel how they'd made the cold seem palpable and evoked the smell of German bread and powdered coffee. In such a place, a composer had written music for four musicians, himself included, who were imprisoned there and for the four instruments that became available—piano, clarinet, violin, and cello.

On that January 1941 night on which Olivier Messiaen premiered his *Quartet for the End of Time* in the so-called concert hall of Stalag VIIIA, my father was selling X-ray film in the Midwest, months before basic training in the heat of Lubbock, Texas. Several inches of snow fell in Indiana that night. I imagine him in some hotel, poring over sales reports and wondering how the war would affect his fledgling career. In Germany that evening, twenty inches of snow covered the ground around the sentry posts and latrines, the coal sheds and cookhouses. Two hundred miles east, thousands of Polish intellectuals—though not yet the Jews—at Auschwitz awaited their fate. The end of the war was still four years away.

In temperatures below zero, the wounded at Stalag VIIIA shivered on stretchers at the feet of the German guards who took up the front rows and, from all accounts, felt an odd pride in the evening's event. Behind them, prisoners—journalists, clergy, carpenters, chefs, many without an iota of interest in chamber music—squirmed on their benches, perhaps hoping for a diversion, something to relieve the monotony of another hour of Ping-Pong or bridge. Messiaen made a few introductory remarks and sat down at the piano; then Henri Akoka picked up his clarinet and put it to his mouth, while Étienne Pasquier and Jean Le Boulaire lifted their bows. The barracks filled with trills, harmonies, solos, melodies, harsh chords, discordances, unfamiliar rhythms. They went on for almost an hour.

In a camp newsletter circulated shortly after the concert, a prisoner known only as V.M. praised the premiere and concluded, *What is crucial following such music is not to fall back to where one is, but onto what one is.*

To "fall back to where one is" would have meant walking out of the concert hall, such as it was, and back into the guarded yard of a German POW camp. And that's exactly where the reviewer—whoever he was—and Messiaen himself went, along with several hundred other men held captive there.

But V.M., and evidently many of the hundreds huddled in barrack 27 who'd just listened to the premiere of what became known as a masterpiece, also felt *moved.* Lifted from the confines of the camp and transported to some other place. Paradise, I can hear Messiaen saying. Some place beyond the constraints of time. *Submit ecstatically,* the composer writes in his preface to the score, *to a vortex, a dizzying interpenetration of superhuman sounds and colors. These fiery swords, these rivers of blue-orange lava, these sudden stars: Behold the cluster, behold the rainbows!*

That'd be a good sight to see, I suppose, especially if the alternative were barbed wire and guard towers. Unlike Messiaen, however, for V.M., the music's imperative evidently had little to do with glimpsing eternity and more to do with landing *onto what one is*—which seems a more interesting place than paradise, if only we could figure out what he meant. Is he suggesting that *what one is* exists as some kind of deep entity—like a soul, peculiarly ours—from which we sometimes depart and to which we sometimes return? Even if such a singular "one" exists, would we, after music had taken us elsewhere, really want return to it? And could we?

I have no idea how my father would have answered that question; V.M., lost to history, can't clarify the phrase he used in his review, and Messiaen himself wasn't interested in existential concerns, at least not secular ones. The music, he claimed, was inspired by his reading of the book of Revelation, in which the seventh angel descends and declares, *There should be time no longer*. From all accounts, the devoutly Catholic composer understood this phrase to mean the aftermath of the Apocalypse and the beginning of eternity. Even those of us who don't put much stock in the everlasting can understand the occasional need to escape our immediate surroundings, especially if they're bound by barbed wire. V.M., in fact, went on in his review to claim that the *Quartet* was a *revenge on captivity, mediocrity, and above all, on ourselves*. Huddled on a bench on that January night in 1941, he must have heard fury in Messiaen's work, a call to arms, a barely sheathed wish to rise up and triumph over . . . what? Hitler? The goons in the towers? The prisoners' own helplessness?

No, Messiaen, would have replied calmly. None of that. The music had nothing to do with needing a way out of Stalag or responding to the horrors of that time but with celebrating what he believed with all his heart would someday arrive. Believe in God, he would have said, and listen to the music, though some of the POWs, rising from their cold wooden benches that night three-quarters of a century ago, weren't sure if what they'd just heard was, in fact, music. Even the three other musicians, violinist Le Boulaire confessed, couldn't quite say what it was they were playing as they strained to make their instruments reach notes and hammer rhythms they'd never attempted before.

Ontological and aesthetic questions aside, however, those who listened—reluctant, stirred, perplexed, returned or not to some sense of themselves, whatever that means—responded similarly that night: with silence. No immediate applause after the final notes of the violin faded inside the barrack, no fidgeting on benches or cots, no blowing into cupped hands to relieve the cold. The notes lingered among the stilled prisoners and their German guards alike. *It was*, the cellist Pasquier declared, *miraculous*.

Indeed.

My father spoke very little about his seventeen months in the camp. Growing up, I don't remember any tension about this silence; it was, I assumed, a clear choice on his part to leave the past behind. Once, however, during a rare visit from my paternal grandparents, they spread the contents of a yellowed envelope on the kitchen table—clippings from wartime newspapers. Picking up one headlined, "Lt. Hurd Listed Lost in Action," my white-haired grandfather bent over the table and wept, and I, who'd never seen a grown man's tears, was embarrassed. My mother kept drying dishes; my father was elsewhere in the house. My grandfather soon straightened his back, blew his nose, and stuffed the clippings back in the envelope. Nobody said a thing.

I began my quest soon after that, reading books about German POW camps—thousands of words describing the camps, the guards, the daily routines. I studied photographs, and when *The Great Escape* was released, I saw it five times in the summer of 1963 so that by the time I had graduated from high school I had cobbled together a detailed landscape of that place about which my father had spoken so little. By my early twenties I had those years of his life choreographed on an imagined stage I could examine whenever I needed to. And I did, each time I tried to understand his relentless optimism, his faith, his habit of calling long distance after I'd grown up and asking if I were okay in a tone that made me picture him hunching his way toward a latrine on a winter night or flattening a tin can into a cooking utensil. "Yes," I'd say to him, "yes, of course, yes, I'm just fine." For a long while, I shrugged through those superficial queries, our lack of intimacy, forgave him his silence about a time that must have helped form who he became. I'd fill in the blanks with borrowed images, imagine I was imagining him well enough.

But at Penn Alps that evening, as the pianist settled on his bench and then the clarinetist coaxed those first six solo notes into the air, I knew I was encountering, perhaps for the first time, something that might depict that absence without images or words, that might help me feel what surely my father and thousands of other captured troops must have felt during the monotony of their endurance. Time is sadness and tedium, Messiaen says. *Time*, my father admits only once in his letters, *lies heavy on our hands.*

Those first notes sound tentative and—I know this sounds ridiculous—then brave. They break the silence that surrounds all music and climb toward a trill while the piano enters and reminds, reminds. For years, I had been able to picture him marking off pages on some sort of calendar, writing yet another postcard home: *My spirit is okay so don't worry about me.* But now it was as if I could feel the heaviness beneath the determination not to give in, could almost hear the sound of his thin-soled boots on the wooden barrack's floor. A few measures later, when the clarinet imitates the black-bird song, the crows on the spruce branch outside the Penn Alps's window became the blackbirds that Messiaen heard, which became the birds my father must have tilted his head back to watch as they flew, unimpeded, over the fences. *A halo of trills*, Messiaen scribbled, notating the high-octave "A" over and over while the piano thuds its low G-flats, and my father tries to reassure his parents in another postcard home: *I am well*, he insists; *keep your chins up.*

The birds, wrote Messiaen, *are the opposite of Time. They are our desire for light, for stars, for rainbows and for jubilant outpourings of song!* Their freedom had nothing to do, he claimed, with Stalag VIII, with the fences and guards. Nor, evidently, did his curious use of palindromes—those rhythms that, played forward or backward, remain the same. But I heard them that night at Penn Alps as pacing, as Messiaen's feet and my father's, back and forth in the crowded barracks, the notes forward and backward on the lines of the staff, the movement so reminiscent of Rilke's panther pacing in its cage: *to him the world is bars, a hundred thousand / bars, and behind the bars, nothing.* No, Messiaen would have said, because such despair was as unthinkable to him as it seemed to have been to my father, who writes in another postcard home: *Memorial Day is beautiful here. I'm getting quite a tan.*

Weeks after the concert at Penn Alps, I opened a large envelope that had arrived in the mail and pulled out the sheet music I'd ordered. Bar lines, double bar lines, ledger lines, and grand staffs. The score for the *Quartet* is fifty-two pages long. I took it to musician friends who tried to help me clap the beats in a Messiaen measure as if I were in grade school again. "Here," I said to one, dropping the score on her lap, "help me count just half a page of the piano." She leaned over the pages, started clapping and counting, *one and two and* . . . and then stopped, studied the page, had to start over. Part of the problem is that only three of the eight movements have time signatures. How then is the pianist to know how many beats a note is worth and how many beats Messiaen wants per measure? What is it, finally, that Messiaen is trying to do with rhythm?

———

Rhythms are a way of organizing emotions. They suggest arrangements and variations of nuanced feelings, a subtle shift, say, from guilt to shame, or the jitter between feeling cherished and owned. A part of me wants to feel Messiaen's work that way too: that his invention and use of what he called "non-retrogradable rhythms" and "isorhythms" was an emotional reaction to the monotonous months of captivity where daily rations of dark bread and water made up the one relentless rhythm in the many months of too much time. Who could blame him for wanting any meter that countered the dreary humdrum of *where he found himself*?

But Messiaen denied that too. In fact, to him, rhythms seem less a musical expression of emotion and more an attempt to transcend time itself in a place. Meter, after all, suggests a regular beat, and what he wanted was the opposite: rhythms to remind us that beyond the bars is an *un*measured eternity—paradise. And as for the specific phrase "the end of time"? He meant it, he said, in two ways, neither of which had anything to do with Stalag: the end of predictable rhythms that bored him and the end of our time here on earth, which tired him.

Regardless, what I, hearing the music that night at Penn Alps, felt was both the monotony I imagined my father must have felt and his resistance to it, his refusal to give in: *Being a prisoner is not so bad . . . it somehow does you good.* I heard in those tangled rhythms of Messiaen's something other than what the composer claimed and what my father said he felt; I heard denial, suppression. I heard the determined banishing of despair in the face of misery. And from my father—who had left a beautiful bride back in the States—not a word about loneliness. *Everything still fine with me.*

After that night at Penn Alps, I hauled out the box of letters and reread them all. *Mild weather is permitting us to play softball already*, he wrote in February 1944. My father was careful with language; he insisted on proper grammar and punctuation. I tried reading his words aloud, listening for rhythms, for nuance—I couldn't hear it—and for the unsaid, which I heard everywhere. How does one, no matter how chipper, fashion a rhythm out of silence and monotone? Perhaps the rhythm of my father's life, then, was exactly that: steady, full of repetitions, controlled. No chance for sudden fluctuations, unpredictable outbursts or retreats. If on the back stage of my father's emotional life some wild man with cymbals and a bass drum waited for a chance he never got, I don't know about it. Only twice in my life did I ever witness even so sharp an emotion as impatience. My father was good natured and amiable. He counted his blessings and did his job, advancing from X-ray sales to photo products manager, performed civic duties, found joy, and kept the curtain closed on whatever darkness his time in captivity might have festered. How can I not be grateful?

The problem, of course, is that I miss him, that man I didn't know. And though Messiaen helped me to imagine my father more emotionally, he also complicated my wish to know more about those years by exemplifying the paradoxical power of denial. Was it really possible to compose for months and keep the work unaffected by the constancy of barbed wire and meager rations, the threat of a guard's capricious whims, the fate of those nearby in

Auschwitz? How much did Messiaen know? How much did he not want to know? And what happens when we refuse to acknowledge what Jungians would call the shadow side?

Or is the work affected anyway, regardless of what the composer believes? Perhaps even enriched by what he does not acknowledge?

Since that night at Penn Alps, I've hit the button on the CD player at home and listened to the *Quartet* dozens of times. And to the sixth movement, "Dance of Fury," more often than that. Its ominous tone comes, in part, from all four instruments playing in lockstep unison. There's no violin trill interrupting the cello, no piano runs bisecting the clarinet's melody. Listening to it, I'm not even sure I can say there is a melody. Instead, all four musicians play all their harsh notes at the exact same time, as if the notes themselves—plucked, blown, and hammered—from all four instruments were marching rigidly in step, increasingly high goosed, building to frantic, feverish trumpeting and gong.

I confess it creeps me out, makes me feel as if a large four-headed body is lurching my way. Describing that sixth movement, Messiaen urges us to think of *music of stone, formidable sonority, movement as irresistible as steel*. I do, and it scares me. It's the danger of thinking about *what one is* when *one* means single minded, which can also mean close minded, both of which can lead to Nazis high-stepping in the streets of Berlin and tanks crushing their way through European villages as they did in the months before my father bailed out of his B-24 over Italy and wound up in Stalag III not far from where Messiaen's masterpiece was premiered. Listening to that movement over and over, I try to imagine resisting a force such as violent righteousness, terror, or even boredom. Perhaps I, too, would have eased myself into a denial I could decide to live with.

———

To touch an ivory key on the piano of my youth was to sit up a little taller, to smooth my skirt, to practice simplified arrangements of Bach's "Minuet" and the manners of a young lady. Though there's something sadly quaint about the old belief that a young woman who couldn't play a simple sonata would never catch a husband, there's something elegant about ivory itself, about its subtle grains and inviting smoothness. Ivory is cool, translucent, a symbol of luxury once used for combs and bracelets, umbrella handles, even the manger of Caligula's favorite horse. I remember prying a loose one up once, holding it to the sun. I could almost see through it. It was how I once imagined a person's life should be—the beautiful made possible by the barely visible grain.

As a child, I knew nothing of ivory's origins; I'd loved it simply for its feel and texture, a thin slice of the exotic that might lead to music. By the time I first heard Messiaen's piece, I knew, of course, what brutality had brought those keys to the genteel parlors of 1890s America. What I'd only recently learned was what complicated system of denial had allowed it all to happen.

Two months before I heard the concert at Penn Alps, I'd gone to Deep River, Connecticut, to research the history of ivory and any ancestors who might have been involved in its production. Connecticut is full of Hurds; there's Hurd State Park and Hurd Brook, Hurds in every city of the state. And I did indeed discover one George C. Hurd who'd worked in the ivory factories in Deep River, but the family history in Deep River was brief—no way to know if he'd been a cutter, a sorter, a grader, or a trader who'd gone to Zanzibar in search of the purest tusks. I did learn that he'd worked in the ivory factories for forty years, had fallen ill in his early seventies, and died at age seventy-seven. Other than that, I found almost nothing about him.

I found plenty, though, about the town's complicated connection to ivory and a man named George Read, who stood at the center of that connection.

In old photographs, Read looks like a stern version of Dr. Welby, who'd also been an imagined, though lesser, father figure to me. Read's forehead is high; white hair curls behind his ears. He gazes straight at the camera through small wire-rimmed glasses. One eye droops a bit. It's hard to imagine him smiling. He is one of the reasons my father bought that old upright I had as a kid. Read had founded one of the two factories in southern Connecticut to which 90 percent of Africa's ivory was shipped. He lived there in the 1800s, built a factory, hired my distant relative, and oversaw the ivory cutters who fondled and caressed the tusks, working like men in love.

A small replica of a Deep River bleach house now stands behind the historical society's building on Main Street. Ten feet by maybe thirty, it looks like a small A-frame greenhouse and was, in fact, designed to maximize sunlight. It had never, though, housed geraniums or green peppers. For years the shelves of bleach houses propped up thousands of small slabs of ivory, exposing them to sunlight for thirty days to whiten their surfaces, transforming them from slivers of elephant tusk to the pearly coverings on piano keys, such as those that Messiaen played with such fervor that January night in 1941. About those slivers in the bleach house, George Read hummed, *Oh Plates lift up your sides and sing praises for this day. Will the Sun Whiten ye up, and ye shall become as the driven snow.* Hymnlike, exultant, the words reflect the fervor with which the ivory industry transformed the small town and made Read and the other ivory producers industry captains who remained committed to the proliferation of piano and piano music throughout America. Cheap ivory meant cheap keyboards, and it wasn't long before a piano in every parlor became a sign of America's well-being. The sheet music industry boomed, Ignacy Jan Paderewsky stormed the country, and young girls like me sat gracefully on benches, smoothed our skirts, and lifted our clean hands.

Read was also a staunch abolitionist. At the corner of North Main and Winter Avenue in Deep River, a small plaque proclaims,

> Led by George Read, Founder of the Town's Ivory Industry,
> Deep River Became Known in the 19th century as "All
> Abolitionist" and a Refuge for Runaway Slaves on the
> Underground Railroad.

The town is obviously proud of Read's abolitionist activity. At a time when slavery was still legal in Connecticut, he unshackled southern slaves, hid them in his home, and helped at least one to change his name, buy property, and live decently in a country torn apart by racism.

Meanwhile, his company relied on African slaves to transport the ivory from Africa's interior to Zanzibar, just off the coast. Only the strongest could carry a hundred pounds of ivory on his back for miles through the jungle without succumbing to disease or starvation or the misery of hopelessness. The survival rate on those treks was, by some estimates, only 25 percent. The rest collapsed; the caravans stepped over them, left in their wake a fifty-year swath of pillage and slaughter. The explorer Henry Morton Stanley lamented, *Every tusk, piece, and scrap in the possession of an Arab trader has been steeped and dyed in blood.*

Seven thousand miles from Deep River and forty years earlier, Livingstone once heard the slaves singing and chanting and reported that their songs celebrated the prospect of life after death, though it was hardly the afterlife Messiaen had in mind, rapturous that *There shall be time no longer.* What they looked forward to, one former slave explained, was returning to murder those who'd sold them and loaded their backs, those whose swords sliced through the weak who'd stumbled and fallen.

The numbers are staggering: for every tusk hauled out of Africa, five natives perished or were sold into slavery; for every pound of ivory, someone died. All told, the piano production that made Deep River and neighboring Ivoryton boom cost two million Africans their lives.

Meanwhile, in Deep River, George Read unshackled another southern slave, founded the local Baptist Church, treated his employees well, helped hundreds of immigrant workers find good jobs and decent housing, built up communities, and placed an order for fifty more tons of ivory.

And the cost of ivory wasn't paid in just human blood. Every tusk also meant an elephant had been speared, hamstrung, shot, poisoned, or bombed. In 1840, even before the heyday, at least a dozen elephants a week were slaughtered for Connecticut factories alone.

So voracious was the western and European appetite for ivory that by the late 1800s, more than thirty-five thousand are estimated to have been slaughtered every year.

In an interview with a local historian that April day in Deep River, I pressed this question: Didn't they know, on some level, where the ivory came from, how it got to Deep River?

"No," he replied.

"And if I searched every volume in this library's archives, I'd find no hint of knowledge, no suggestion of repression, no secret awareness of denial?"

"No," he replied.

And when I did, he was right.

If anyone had directly asked him a century ago if he knew how the ivory that graced his company's keyboards landed in Deep River, Read would have uttered, "No."

Asked whether his music had anything to do with the camp, Messiaen declared, "No."

When his worried parents wrote to ask whether his spirits were low, my father answered, "No."

———

At Penn Alps that evening, after the last notes of the violin faded and the musicians bowed and exited and returned and bowed again, I walked out into the balmy July evening and got into my car and took detour after detour home, driving north first on a pot-holed road that runs along the banks of the Casselman River and then east over a forested ridge, southwest through farmlands, seeing that, for me, movement had taken a literal form: I wanted to travel, to watch the scenery change. To do what Messiaen couldn't do when he composed his masterpiece, what my father couldn't do during those months at Stalag, what Read perhaps should have done, especially if the scenery included the tusk-strewn streets of Zanzibar.

I wandered the way I remember doing with my parents when I was a child and my father would get behind the wheel and we'd meander north from Boston into New Hampshire, maybe Maine, down the coast, the point being movement, not destination, or, more to the point, my point being that perhaps my father, too, needed to keep moving, that his months in a POW camp not far from Messiaen's might have instilled a restlessness. How, I'd like to ask my father now, might you have reacted to Messiaen's music if he'd been in your camp, if he and his musicians had mounted a stage in Stalag III and performed that piece? Would you have felt uplifted? Moved *to what one is?*

My father was not a music lover. His letters from Stalag III describe hockey, basketball, occasional theater. He loved physical enterprise, not emotional adventure. On his first combat mission, he reports he felt no *pre-game nervousness.* And though he says he wondered about other men's thoughts, he admits that he himself felt *no particularly different feeling than when going on a mission in the States. I was more interested in what combat would be like than excited or scared.* Crossing the Mediterranean Sea after having abandoned the original target and dropped six thousand pounds of bombs on the center of some Italian town, he acknowledges that at the end of his first mission, *My chief impression was that I was cold and sleepy.*

My father's letters are full of weather reports and lists of the people who sent him cards. The few emotional phrases (*my darling wife, my dear wife*) read like place markers, obligatory insertions, memos to self. My father would never pour his heart out on the page. He'd make a lousy memoirist. Even in the midst of the infamous March of Death from Stalag III to Mooseberg, his diary reads, *Weather balmy—just right for walking without overcoats.* The horrors evidently never destroyed his spirit. Who's to say such denial—personal, benign—isn't useful?

The problem, as I said before, is that I miss him. I miss knowing the rest of the man who became my father. Even reading the thousands of pages on Stalag III and poring over his correspondence doesn't bring to me the man I never knew and miss regardless, the part of him who had, perhaps, disappeared too far into silence. In Eugene Drucker's book *The Savior,* imprisoned Jews talk about *what it takes to stay alive from one day to the next, but we can't talk about what it feels to be here. They've taken away our language—I mean the language of the heart.*

My father believed in good deeds; I don't even know if he had a language of the heart. We were not intimates. And I, of course, was doomed to learn from him the value of a private life, my own secrets well closeted, intimacy a careful choice—never an obligation—to open that door a crack. It's been decades since that war ended, since Messiaen was freed and most POWs, including the man who became my father, returned home, years now since they died. But sometimes when I sit in my study and replay the *Quartet* and hear those soaring violin notes, I feel closer to him than I ever did when he was alive and wiring my house or teaching me to trim the jib as we sailed across Chesapeake Bay. And when those piano chords in the last movement slowly heartbeat their way up the keyboard and the violinist coaxes those high higher notes from full sound to fine spun and weightless, I feel myself leaning forward, straining even, to hear the sounds as they thin to tendril and seem to take me toward him, *no longer caught*, as the poet Goethe says, *in the obsession with darkness. Distance*, he goes on,

> does not make you falter,
> now, arriving in magic, flying,
> and, finally, insane for the light,
> you are the butterfly and you are gone.

The violin, barely audible now, slides into a high-octave E and, quivering, holds that last note until it vanishes.

What other than silence could possibly follow that?

Eternity, Messiaen insists, and perhaps that's what his listeners longed for that night, so long as he didn't mean there in that camp.

Heaven, my father would have said.

More silence, I propose.

Forgiveness, George Read might have suggested.

But Goethe isn't finished:

        . . . so long as you haven't experienced
        this: to die and so to grow
        you are only a troubled guest
        on the dark earth.

Until transcendence—I can hear Goethe's voice rising now, becoming more urgent—you are merely transient and disquieted. And afterward, the reviewer V.M. might interject, perhaps exultantly, you have a chance to return to what you really are.

Which is what? Goethe, too, might have asked, calming himself, settling back into his leather chair, lighting a pipe, speaking across the centuries. *What one are you?*

George Read, grand patriarch of Deep River, was described as a quiet man. Asked once if he knew what the townspeople whispered about him, he denied a specific allegation and then muttered, *But I do worse things.*

Claiming the *Quartet* had nothing whatsoever to do with hardships of captivity, Messiaen titled the sixth movement "Dance of Fury."

In a postcard that begins, *We manage to have some enjoyment and quite a few laughs*, my father concludes, *No mail yet—anxious to hear from you.* And when my sister sat on his deathbed and praised him for being such a good, good man, he whispered, "No, no, I'm not."

What one are you?

To enter the Addo Elephant Preserve in South Africa, you must pass by a pair of tuskless elephant skulls positioned by the gate. I went there some months after I began to listen to the *Quartet* and to think about ivory, in part to watch the giant animals lumber through the African thicket. I tried to imagine shooting one, wrestling the tusk from the bone, lugging it for miles to the coast.

At the Addo entrance gate, I got out of the car and ran my hands over the larger of the cool, bony skulls. With the guard's help, I could see how far into the skull the tusk had been embedded and why George Read's hunters farther north would have learned to wait a few days after they'd killed one so that the tusks would begin to loosen as the body began to decay and they'd be less likely to have to resort to pulleys and chains to yank them free. I eased my hand a foot deep into the skull's cavity that had once held the ivory, feeling as if this tangible reminder of pillage and death were the real entrance to Addo, the lives of the elephants, and the history of piano keys. Perhaps this is what Messiaen's *Quartet* does too: ushers me into what is not just my father's silence or anything else as singular as that but into the sweep of triumphs we've achieved and messes we've made. Surrounded by carnage and music, we see ourselves for what we are; we become, in other words, exactly what Goethe criticizes: troubled guests. Goethe, of course, is chiding us: *Only that?* he asks, urging us onward. But *that*, in fact, seems like plenty and might be a noble enough goal: to live here for a while as troubled guests, aware that we are each part of a humanity that has been brutal and noble, that we are makers of small triumphs and failures, and then we are gone.

—~—

The threads that link Messiaen, my father, the ivory trade of Africa, and the genteel community of abolitionists in Connecticut have mostly frayed and disappeared. Hitler is long dead, plastic veneers the piano keys my granddaughter plays, and this country elected a black man as president. But when I lie on the floor of my study and replay the *Quartet* again, the music contains it all: slaughtered tribes and elephant tusks, those skulls at Addo, the somber face of George Read, barbed wire, Messiaen's celebration of eternity, all of which helps me to mostly give up the probing of my father's private life. How much and to whom does it finally matter that Messiaen denied his surroundings, that my father learned not to feel despair? About George Read I'm less sure, though surely any flat-out condemnation would have to be weighed against the many immigrant lives he saved. On my study floor, I've given up, too, trying to track the meter of the opening movement. I give myself over to the intricacies of rhythm, the trills and interruptions, to the complicated insistence of deep piano chords, and to the obvious fact that as individuals, of course, we deserve the right to be private about the times we've felt diminished. It's when denials reach historical dimensions that we're obliged to listen to what hasn't been said.

Perhaps Messiaen provides a return not to what any of us *is* but to what *we are*, to our multiple longings and disappointments and joys, to the whole range of what it means to be human. Though it's hard to love what any of us, in full dimensions, *is*, art often helps formalize that which is elusive and strange; it allows us, if not to love, then to sympathize with, to understand. That the prisoners, wordless in their wool coats that night, were moved is not surprising: the music must have recalled something for them. For me, the music and a moment in history converged and gave form to what I didn't know I'd been missing. The solace I feel when I listen now to the *Quartet* might be different from theirs, more like a finely tuned nostalgia for what I never had.

11

Mile 15

BELOW PEA RIDGE

―――――

Though it's possible to separate a river from its valley, one always shapes the other. Here the Savage meanders, indirect as a series of *what ifs?* The accent is on nuance.

What if I heard the dove's silence as a mocking of my own? Would I be crazy?

What if I said that tiny space between stillness and change is made of air not stone? Would I be wise or stupid?

Early origin of the word *meander*: confusion, intricacies.

―――――

Sounding out a new word, Samantha tries *OBject* and then *obJECT* and looks to me to clarify.

One is a thing, I say; the other, an argument.

What's the difference? she wants to know.

―――――

And which, I'm tempted to ask, is the river?

———————

Meanwhile, in tiny cascades of flutter and tap, hundreds of hemlock needles drop into quiet waters below, and off in the distance a
saw-whet owl whistles over and over again: *too, too, too, too.*

12

Whose Story Is This?

It is not the voice that commands the story: it is the ear.

ITALO CALVINO

The juvenile version of a red-spotted newt looks like a tiny flicker of flame on the forest floor after rain. It's more color than form: orange defines it, simultaneously announces and warns. A toad that's force-fed a diet of efts will die within hours. So will a brook trout. Orange dissuades them but not Samantha, who will soon spy one during our late morning walk.

—

The day has not begun well. Samantha woke up cranky and came reluctantly to the window where I stood listening to the *sweet-sweet/chew-chew* of the indigo buntings whose bodies seemed to gleam in the dark green canopy like little blue-skinned Buddhas. She had no interest in any aura some say surrounds the holy ones or in making small mythologies out of birds. She wanted breakfast: blackberries and toast.

—

The buntings had come from some two thousand miles away, from Mexico, from dry warmth and cactus and the sounds of small insects scritching the ground. At some signal we know little about, they rise one evening in April. Unlike most migrators, they travel at night, twisting their bird-brained heads now and then on the long flight back to check on star patterns, their only clue to finding the summer home in the oaks outside our bedroom. The moral of the story: perseverance, the power of instinct to find home. Or maybe, for us, the delight of that deep blue dotting deep summer green. Isn't pleasure—the getting, losing, and, if we're lucky, redefining of it—one of the world's most basic stories?

——

Or is it metamorphosis? By the time it's three months old, the eft that began as a larva in the pond to which it will someday return as a newt has clambered ashore, grown a pair of lungs, blushed its skin to deep orange, and dotted it with black-bordered red spots that resemble bull's-eyes or portals, depending on whether I'm thinking about focus (look *there*) or vision (look *through* it).

I don't usually point out an eft to young kids. Seeing one, I'll note it silently and hope whatever child is with me is too interested in climbing trees or digging holes to notice it thrashing its stubby legs to get out of our way. An eft, though, has likely by now paused in the middle of the trail by the river where, in a few minutes, it will sense the earth begin to tremble. Earless, it will "hear" with its body that a woman and child are approaching.

——

Outside, at the edge of the yard, the cyclical *sweet-sweet/chew-chew* of indigo buntings continued, the notes short and bright, quick coupled phrases. Delicate, thin, light. Not a bird of full notes but flute-like, airy, a trapeze pairing of notes above the perennial bee balm and clover, among raucous crow calls. A blur of blue, it sings, back and forth between the nest it weaves and the source of its materials: the field we walk in, bark debris, deer hair snagged on hawthorn, leaf bits from under maples. The bird collects, shapes, inhabits. The nest is not a sex place; it's the necessary aftermath—a half dozen or so out there now, warmed by feathered bodies. Altogether, they might cradle some two dozen eggs above the twig snap of red fox and raccoon, the clump of my boots and Samantha's sneakers. Into and out of them, the blue and the song go on for twelve days.

———

Can we think of birds as having stories? Their lives have narrative arcs, full of conflicts and resolutions; one of them always wants something and is often foiled by something else, and surely now and then a bird plays a minor character keen on disturbing a neighbor's nest. We are the storytellers, of course, not them. They are the ones who merely live out their lives. But to talk of their stories—the egg shards we found on the ground, the mess of feathers, a dense pointillism of bird shit that suggests a conference or a single bird's obsession with, say, the hood of the car—is to help us see the treetops as not just space up there but as arboreal stages in some creatures' drama.

———

Samantha was cranky this morning because last night thousands of katydids seemed to press against the screen of the open window, pulsing their *che-che-che/katydid-katydid* into her restless sleep. Is any other creature so loud with desire? They summon and call, ratchet the evening into high-pitched fever. Disguised as leaves, they chirp in dialects that differentiate a rattler round-winged katydid from a black-legged meadow one. Five-pulsing chirpers want nothing to do with alternating two-three pulsers or with those who sing in longer phrases. What good is desire if it doesn't discriminate?

———

A bunting will rip such a bug apart and drop the morsels into waiting beaks. For it, too, sound would have helped determine mate. Even more attuned to regional dialects than are katydids, buntings who grow up on this western side of the ridge will sing a little differently than their same-species brethren to the east.

———

The path with the eft lies just to the south.

———

"You know how they make that sound?" I asked Samantha last night. "You know how your dad strums his guitar?" Pausing with one hand on the window crank, she turned to scowl at me. One of their front wings, I told her, has a tiny scraper on it. The other is edged with little teeth. "So just like your dad drags his fingers over the guitar strings, the katydid drags the scraper over the tiny teeth. Like this," I added, pulling her into my lap and trying to mimic the action with her arms. "And know where their ears are? Near their knees!" The little tale did nothing to quiet the katydids or to help her sleep more peacefully.

———

A young indigo bunting has two sounds to work with—the one wired into its tiny head and the adult one it hears. Out of its beak, which has until then done nothing but open for food, comes its first warbling attempt. Now it has three sounds to work with: the first two and the hesitant fumbling errors from its own throat. It listens to the latter, learns to distinguish between its own warble and the song the adult makes. I could wonder here about human parallels, but surely one point of a story is to stay in it for a while, to inhabit, not my world, but the other's—the drama roving audibly above me, chicks in the nest, learning about echo and mimic and what they need to do to keep the song the song.

———

After breakfast, Samantha wanted crayons and paper. "In a minute," I told her. "How about you sit with me and listen for a second? Then maybe you could draw what you hear."

"Draw what I hear?" she asked, frowning at me. "You mean the color?"

———

The buntings' song and the katydids' chirp lack a certain shapeliness. The phrases go on and on. So do Pachelbel's phrases in his *Canon*—no clear beginning, no clear ending, melodically static, the same phrases played with only minor variation over twenty times. No counterpoints or culminations, no slow buildup or final flourish, and yet one of the most popular pieces played at weddings all over the country for decades. Shall I mention that weddings—those supposed starts of new stories—might need as background the continuing story of the *Canon*, might need, in fact, the reassurance of a formlessness that does not intimate an ending?

And that Balinese lovers often forgo sexual climax? They're practiced in the fine art of lingering, of floating in the plateau of almost, almost.

That music's power can be heightened when the chords do not quickly resolve?

That John Cage once said, *More and more I have the feeling that we are getting nowhere. Slowly, as the talk goes on, we are getting nowhere and that is a pleasure?*

Don't let anyone tell you these unresolved interludes have nothing to do with stories. If they make us impatient, it's likely because we can't hear them as chapters or grace notes.

———

For us, listening, there's no tension in the buntings' song, no tightening of suspense or need for resolution. While they're here for the summer, the narrow border between lawn and field is brushed full of their couplets. In August the katydids fill up the night. On hot evenings they ramp up the tempo; on cooler nights: *ritardando.* They slow it down. The songs, like most animals' songs—including ours—are a long sequence of variation and repeats that feels to me almost kinesthetic, a kind of back and forth rhythm that has the power to console: *Repeat the sounding joy.*

———

Or *Repeat the sounding woe*: owl screech, rabbit shriek, fire crackle, storm, any variety of the sounds that signal *finis*.

———

Ten minutes later, Samantha's drawings littered the dining room table—big swirls of color and wavy lines. "So," my husband asked her, picking one up, "what are these?" Samantha has a way of throwing her hands in the air and jutting her head forward in exasperation to remind you that the question you've just asked is really stupid.

"They're people!" she declared.

"Doing what?" he asked.

"Duh, Pop! This is the mom, and this is the kid, and they're going to go to the circus, but then . . ." she hesitated, frowning at the paper, "the ice cream melted."

———

Which is why we are on this damp river path when she spots the one thing I don't want her to see. There's a story behind my caution. As a six-year-old, my son once carried a couple of efts home from the woods, opened the spring-loaded door on an exterior electrical socket, and snapped their tails behind it.

My nephew too: back from a walk one day, he emptied his pockets on the porch, addressed them by name—crooning Spotty or Flame—as they hurried to the edge, only to be corralled back into his makeshift paddock of twigs and stones.

So what that efts—lifted up, even pocketed—can use the earth's magnetic field to find their way back home? No sympathy for wrenching dislocation? I issued a prohibition and quit pointing them out. Better, I decided, that they go unnoticed than be subjected to too much interference. The kids' ignorance might then become the bliss of efts, though such a strategy carries the risk of heedless trampling. And worse: the world made smaller.

———

We are trailing stories, she and I—mine about the recent death of a friend; hers, maybe, about katydids or ice cream—and even as we walk this late morning, their timbre lingers. The best stories don't really end; they leave the door ajar, nudge us to listen to the ways they do and do not merge with ones we've carried around for years.

Repetition & variation: the calm manic music, the poet Ted Deppe notes, *of one who belongs here*. Isn't *how* to belong here—whether *here* means on this damp trail or among the songs and groans and silences of a full or empty heart—the story we keep trying to rewrite? And because *here* surely means, at its truest, not *just* here, aren't we always in the business of splicing storylines? Trying to enlarge the mesh in which we're caught?

For these two weeks every August, the katydid chorus overlaps the buntings' song while the efts crawl up the trail along the river and the breakdown of chlorophyll begins to ungreen the leaves. Soon the birds will head south. As nighttime temperatures plummet, we will close the windows, and the katydids will freeze to death. Secreted in the barky folds of the oaks, though, thousands of eggs will wait until spring: chapter 362, verse 5003. It seems no single story that doesn't suggest the continuing existence of other stories can ever be sufficient.

Samantha's young, so her stories are fewer, but when she spies the eft on the trail, I hear a new one in the making: "A dragon!" she breathes, "headed right for the princess." Her world is full: monsters press against open windows, heroes rescue a neighbor's dog, the plastic gargoyles she marches around my garden protect a queen I've never seen.

As we squat on the path to study the stubby orange legs, a big maple leaf, one of dozens already falling on this late summer day, lands smack on top of it, darkening its world. For a moment the princess is safe. So is the eft.

But that's not the end.

Later, over Cheerios, she asks if the eft will stay beneath the leaf. One answer would be a story about danger; the other, about escape. Of course not, I think. Yes, I say.

13

Mile 20

AT THE CONFLUENCE WITH ELK LICK

—~~~—

Samantha marches right to the tributary's edge, holds up her right palm, and commands, "Stop!"

—~~~~—

I don't know enough to finish this story or even to know if this is a story, not just a phase in some monotonous do-it-again-over-and-over watery drama of let's see what happens next.

Sometimes rivers remind us of their powers; other times, of our powerlessness.

—~~~~~—

Hundreds of starlings swoop low through the trees, rustling like big black leaves in late summer; only they don't move down, nor with the quiet waft of giving up, giving in, but through—horizontally in and among the trees. For three or four minutes they whoosh, wings flapping, moving the air, even, it seems, the hair on our heads, their feathered bodies like beating bits of a dark dispersed cloud, coming from somewhere, headed somewhere else.

14

Overhearing

Monitoring a river is a bit like eavesdropping on a landscape. Though nothing's covert about it, you have your regular surveillance sites where you crouch by the water, listen to the gurgle that can indicate changes in flow, slip your probe in, take your readings, peer around for any clues of disturbance, and move quietly away. Like any eavesdropper, you're after hints of a bigger story that might secretly be in play—pollution, illegal runoff, clandestine agreements about cover-ups. You send the data in to the group that oversees the monitoring, hope nothing sets off alarms, return in a week or two, take up your position again.

I should confess here that I used to fantasize about being a Peeping Tom. I'm not talking about spying on naked bodies but about listening in on unaware conversationalists. I favored the aural version. I was, so to speak, an Eavesdropping Tom. The notion of crouching at someone's window, overhearing random bits of talk, gathering snippets of phrases and rearranging them into full-blown stories appealed to me when I was young. It is, I suppose, a natural tendency; we do it all the time—at parties and cafés, among friends, and for we who monitor, here at edge of the river. There's something satisfying about trying to stitch bits of evidence together into some narrative whole that might enlarge the picture, make the drama more true.

An hour ago I'd been snooping, if I may use that word, at the confluence of Mud Lick and the Savage River, one of my regular monitoring sites. The river had been clear, I noted, the temperature, conductivity, and dissolved solids readings all within typical range. Nothing suggested shady business or subversive activity going on upstream. I signed the forms, washed the equipment, stashed it in the car, retied my boots, and headed north—not for surveillance but for pleasure.

If you follow the Savage River upstream from that confluence with Mud Lick, you wind for a while through state forest thick with rhododendron and hemlock and then out into open meadows. And now, in full view—no secrets here—is a red-winged blackbird singing his heart out. Some describe his song as *conk-a-ree, conk-a-ree.* To me, it's more like a couple of low notes followed by a fast high trill flattened slightly by what I imagine might be the fatigue of the eight-hundred-mile journey here.

He's one of a large flock of males who arrived in this area last week. They'd been scouting the meadows, eyeing the grasses for nest sites, readying themselves for the females who flew in a few days later. On the swaying stalk the male puffs his wings, flashes his red epaulets, signaling, *here, here.*

Blackbirds, the composer Olivier Messiaen claims, often sing whimsically, cheerfully. In his "Le Merle Noir" ("The Blackbird") the pianist and flutist play rippling runs and high trills, stopping and starting some phrases, repeating others. Birdsong, the composer said, represents our desire for transcendence and light. His is a religious hearing. His, I might propose, is an example of piling onto the blackbird's song a whole host of associations. It's a practice I know well.

When I was a child, I believed that sunbeamed clearings in dark woods marked the places where God had lowered an invisible stairway. There was such a spot not far from my childhood home, large and wet enough for frogs and efts and a girl's obsession with the possibility of underlying song, some "music of the spheres" that might suggest a universal coherence. I don't remember whether I hoped he would come down or I might go up, but I'd stand there, barefoot in the mud and motionless, praying for a purity I never managed to feel.

Ordinary experiences have eroded those beliefs, though not the sense that listening well is one way to make sense of the world. It isn't that I want more sound, more song. I think what I want is better ability to discriminate among the varieties—finer gradations, clearer distinctions, better discernment, which is why I, standing in front of the red-winged blackbird, have little patience today for reverence. I've grown wary of that practice of overzealous connecting of snippets we've gleaned from eavesdropping.

Overhearing, I might call it now, meaning we're more likely hearing our own minds at work and not the bird itself.

Decades from childhood now, I consider myself a devout agnostic, by which I mean that—concerning the gods and knowable futures—I aim to relinquish my need for certainties and simple answers. Though I'm still drawn to sunlit clearings like this one where the blackbird sings, I know now it was likely made by farming decades ago. I don't revere it. Nor do I revere the Savage River gurgling nearby, nor the forest itself, nor the mountains I've explored for forty years, nor the rocky shores of Maine, drawn as I am to their creviced granite and sprays of spume. In fact, I no longer revere "nature." Maybe that's *because* of how I've spent those decades. My father used to ask when I'd return, fingernails dirty, knees scraped, pockets full of mosses or stones, "Were you out communing with nature?" Communing? Meaning *to converse familiarly*? No. Even if I ever tried, nothing out there ever answered. Nor was I in *communion*, as in *to partake of the sacrament*.

And *out there* wasn't "nature," which is, of course, an abstract noun, an idea. To revere a construct of the human mind seems to me now an exercise in narcissism.

What's out here along the river this afternoon isn't "nature" but swaths of ferns, at least three popping grasshoppers, a scurrying mouse, the ordinary squish of boot on rotten logs, all the unseen: zillions of microbes, fungi, and woodlice converting dead grasses to humus. And now a red-winged blackbird singing. What is there to revere? They have their lives, worked out over millennia, their robustness and ill health, dependencies and ruthless urges to stay alive. I might admire, even marvel (all those rotifers beating their cilia to swim across a film of water on a leaf!), but to worship, it seems to me, is to idolize; to revere is to elevate, which means to separate. I don't wish any more distance between "nature" and me than has, by virtue of the culture I was born into, already been driven deep enough between us.

And so here I am, trying to undo the single-mindedness of reverence, the uncomplicated veneration that can tighten, vice-like, when one begins to doubt. I could tell you now about the day I saw—as most of us have—a crow on the side of the road beak-deep in a groundhog's innards, or the fawn's stillness as a coyote approached, even the shredded bark on an oak stump that meant a shrew had swept dozens of beetles into its gullet.

The temptation to make *more* of who we are and where we live, what we hear and see and touch, seems endemic. I don't wish to argue for less but for the sufficiency of the marvelous complexity of what's so richly and palpably *here and now*.

———

"How about trusting the music itself?" Betty once chided me. Halfway through a lesson one day, I'd been playing the second movement of the Mozart sonata I was scheduled to perform in several months. Gone, for the moment, was my hesitant fumbling, my history of playing with feather fingers, as my mother used to lament. I love that Mozart movement, and I know most of it well. I played it expressively, building crescendos and arriving, secretly pleased, at the top of a run. Hear me? I thought, aware of Betty sitting silently beside me. Hear how well I'm doing here?

When I finished, Betty leaned over and pointed to those exact measures on the score. "Ease off here," she said. "You're overcommunicating. Do you doubt Mozart's ability to make something beautiful? Let the music play itself."

———

And, likewise, the bird his song.

There's something more to doubt (no end to doubt!), and it nags at me. Worship can imply an agreement not to touch or to look too closely. Think of Eve and the apple or Christ's *noli me tangere.* Think of a theology whose deity declares, *My face shall not be seen.* I'm all for bending down, even kneeling, but I want to do it with a magnifying glass in hand, the better to see a centipede licking her eggs to ward off soil fungi, the fungi sending minerals and water to plant roots, the plant returning the favor with a supply of sugars and energy it pulls from the sun.

And what about the supposed harmony of "being one with nature"? A phrase patently false and not solely for those who've ever immersed themselves in the gritty, multibugged, multilayered prodigality of ocean or soil. Do we really want to be "one with" an ichneumon wasp or its victim, as Stephen Jay Gould once observed?

Sun on my shoulders, birdsong, river song in my ears, I want to be done with the deafness that too often accompanies platitudes and bliss. Done, too, with the insulating barrier that reverence inserts between us and what we're hearing, seeing. Surely reverence can warp our attention and thus no longer help us to see and to hear where we live or to talk intelligently about problems we've caused and ways we might begin to solve them. Instead of reverence, wouldn't a caution against overhearing be one way a wisdom of respect might finally evolve?

Let me confess here that along with my childhood proclivity toward the aural version of Peeping Toms, I liked the comfort of feeling reverent—all those Sundays when I could feel good about the future I believed my piety foretold. And even now the deeply satisfying pleasure of listening to this blackbird in the middle of a meadow open his beak and belt out that musical phrase is enough to silence me. But sleuthing ought not to confirm what we already feel; it ought, instead, to test our previous notions of nature or self, families or watersheds. The trouble with a preexisting reverence is that it doesn't trouble us enough into discovery.

Is there an urgency here? In a society in which nearly half of us don't believe in the seriousness of global warming, in which some 40 percent dismiss evolution, what we need is not more reverence, which by its nature seldom inspires clear-eyed investigation. What we need, more than ever, are eavesdropping sleuths driven to scrutinize the uncertainties and to explore, not just extol, the workings of the natural world, the paradoxes and ambiguities of what's happening underfoot and overhead, how things work, how to really see where we are and how to live here. What *is* this sediment muddying the river? What does a chunk of shale split open by fracking actually look like ten thousand feet below the surface of the earth? What does the blackbird's early arrival this spring say about climate change?

If we're lucky, our sleuthing through both beauty and brutality might also be marked by the unexpected arrival smack in the middle of a stance in opposition to the one with which we started. And if that stance, skewered by humor and a sense of complicity, informed by hearing, not *over*hearing, turned out to be—lo and behold!—one of reverence, then it would be a hard-won reverence.

Toward this red-winged blackbird—fiery epaulets, sleek black body, song that ripples and trills—I can almost feel it.

15

Wanting Not to Be Heard

But I didn't want a voice.
I wanted clay that could
be centered on a wheel
MARGARET GIBSON

History is full of the unvoiced pleas of people bullied into silence by brutes. Not being heard, we know, is often a tragedy. But it can also be an artful ploy. There's the toadfish, for example, about to come face-to-face with a dolphin, and there are people like me who occasionally plot to hole up at home like a muted recluse. In not wanting to be heard, the bullied, the toadfish, and I have two things in common: the goal—however accurate or ill conceived—of survival and the risk of getting stuck in silence.

Physical survival was not what I had in mind the Saturday last August when I was trying to tiptoe through the woods along the Savage River with Samantha. Seeing wild turkeys was. We'd been hearing their clucks for twenty minutes, coming from somewhere up the hill a ways, and set off to find them. Toe first, I suggested to her, pressing mine into the damp cushion of leaf debris—better control over how the rest of the foot eases or clumps on the forest floor. But Samantha wasn't much interested in stealthy stalking and leapt from rock to rock, squealing with every landing. And the turkeys themselves seemed to have no interest in a noisy threat drawing near. They neither silenced themselves nor fled. Instead, they kept up their clucking until we got too close, and then they bumped and banged into the air in a sudden racket of clumsy wing flopping.

With them was probably a passel of poults just learning to fly. And nearby, a Virginia possum, hungry and silent.

Toadfish are better than turkeys at eluding predators. Cruising the warm waters of the Gulf of Mexico, they use their swim bladders to emit a high-pitched come-hither whistle to potential mates. But detecting the low-pitched pops of a hungry dolphin nearby, the toadfish goes silent. To the dolphin, who hunts in part by listening, a soundless toadfish, even within sight, is as good as hidden. Adaptive silence, scientists call it: the ability to stay visible while disappearing into muteness when danger threatens.

Other creatures do it too. The normally vocal terns go mute when skuas, large winged and sharp clawed, prowl overhead. The terns aren't physically hiding their bodies; they're acoustically hiding, avoiding detection by ceasing their usual *kirri-kirri* call. The skuas are flummoxed. Somewhere in their tiny brains, it must look like a tern, move like a tern, but minus the sounds of tern, be something other than tern. Still hungry, the skuas move on to the next stretch of beach or cliff along the shore where covey by covey the terns grow quiet until the danger has passed.

Adaptive silence differs from acoustical camouflage, which involves not just going silent but going silent among other sounds. Hiding, in other words, inside cacophonies or choruses of others, where the discrete sound of an individual vanishes. When an echolocating whale, for example, uses its sonar to detect a squid, the squid can slither among other critters and rocks on the ocean floor. There, close to the setting of its birth, it can lie low while the whale's sonar bounces off less appealing prey or the rocks and muddy bottom. A moth fleeing an echolocating bat flies low among shrubs populated by other bugs until the bat, confused by too many blips on its radar, gives up and goes elsewhere. For all these creatures the point is to hide inside the reverberations and noises of others.

I know this tactic well. My twin is gregarious; my second husband, like my first, is sociable and loves a conversation full of interruptions, lively give-and-take, and bellyful laughter. My history has been to use all three of them to disguise my own reticence, to pro-tect—or do I mean to cover?—my own silences. I'm fond of the word *crypsis* and all its implications: enigmas, subterranean vaults, secret characters. Once, decades ago, at a campground with my first husband, the couple tenting nearby invited us over for beer and chips. My ex is an extrovert, affable and engaging. Among the three of them, a spirited conversation ensued about grant writing, sports, and the care of chickens, while I, torn between wanting to watch the night sky and not to seem a social misfit, sat mute at the campfire's edge. When we got up at last to leave, the woman finally looked at me, smiled, and made some clichéd remark about "still waters run deep." How wrong she was, I thought, smiling at her.

But I like to think that sometimes that cliché might be true—and that choosing silence now and then might sometimes protect us from more than others' fangs or poison darts. Call it the soul, character, the coolness of a developed conscience starved for sub-tlety: some part of us, I'll wager, needs moments like these to sur-vive, needs a break from the expectation—our own and others'—to speak. Beyond the buzz of public spaces and their array of lit-eral and metaphoric microphones, megaphones, and cell phones, beyond even whatever forms those devices take in our own minds, there can emerge a different kind of hospitality. Some room for those unintended thoughts too young yet to be spoken to others. It's there, in that silent room, Rilke says, that Orpheus *built a temple inside their hearing*. Betty, I think, would say something about the silence being the climax of all sound. Silence, I would add, can be an antidote to claustrophobia.

None of this is new.

But there's this from Samantha: "When it's quiet, I like to build a boat." When I asked what she meant, she just looked at me.

And this from the poet Margaret Gibson: *But I didn't want a voice. / I wanted clay that could be centered on a wheel.* For Gibson, I think, silence has to do neither with release into some boundless realm nor with an auditory trapdoor that opens to some inner self. It's a container she's after. The kind that can hold quiet all the way through consolation and out the other side into confrontation—with one's own beliefs, assumptions, fears, with, as she says, *Bits and pieces the dead left behind*: the griefs and angers we cling to, the solaces that keep us stuck.

Make no mistake: I'm not advocating the quiet of comas or near-death experiences. I have no wish for the equivalent of lying mute on the ocean floor until a bigger fish gives up and swims away. Besides, most of us, just by the nature of our mostly ordinary lives, have plenty of experiences being ignored, overlooked, our voices stripped as we're herded into that abyss known as "the American People."

But I'm thinking here that when we inspect ourselves in a cryptic state—as only humans can—we might discern the origins of our pretensions, underneath which usually lie our fears. We might make more possible just the opposite of near-death moments: *near-life* experiences—the paradoxical rush of no-more-hiding that comes from the dismantling of our own clichéd comforts, like that one about still waters.

Because the truth is, still waters can also grow stagnant. One risk of adaptive silence and acoustical camouflage is overdosing on aloneness: be quiet and you reduce the likelihood of being eaten, yes, but you also increase the risk of going friendless, mateless. If you're a frog, your quieter, less complex call might reduce the chance of a hungry bat zeroing in on you, but it also means the sex-driven frog on a nearby lily pad is less likely to leap in your direction. As a human, you risk becoming a wallflower or a stay-at-home shy one whom others feel the need to urge from your shell.

At the end of a lesson one day, Betty pulls out her calendar to confirm a December date for a small performance that would include me and a few of her other students.

"That works for you?" she asks.

I don't answer.

I'd started lessons because I wanted to hear music better. No recitals, I told Betty that first day. It's just you and I and your piano and mine. I want nothing to do with performance. But now, two years in, I'm starting to notice small surges of other pleasures: playing a page now and then without major errors, getting the touches right, the rhythms clear, receiving a compliment from Betty—small steps of progress that any serious musician would take for granted as necessary to mastery. But, me, I'm wrestling with whether they signal a switch from learning to listen to actually wanting to be heard and whether the latter introduces something new, maybe tainted, into this small cocoon I've made for Betty and me and the music.

She reminds me that preparing to play for others might help me go deeper into the music.

"How about just a short performance with a tiny audience of fellow students?"

Nothing until these recent piano lessons has made me look harder at my paradoxical wish for anonymity and recognition. My mantra for years: I love to be invisible and I hate to be ignored. How, then, to settle this looming question of whether to perform or not?

—————

Much of the world survives by hiding, and, luckily, the world is pocked with secret crannies: hollow trees, underground dens, cubbyholes, attics. Most creatures, including us, can find a good spot when we need to. But a possum in the middle of the road last summer reminded me that when such nooks are, for whatever reasons, in short supply or not nearby, even the body itself can become its own hiding place.

After we'd flushed the turkeys into flight, Samantha and I emerged from the canopy of oaks onto a road that cuts southeast along Elk Lick and then south along the Savage River, and there it was, on its side, motionless, in plain view, in a direct line of any traffic.

A possum with its ear to the ground like that isn't interested in being listened to. It is, in fact, doing the opposite: trying to disappear inside its body, trying not to be heard. Tonic immobility, biologists call it: the involuntary state of paralysis some animals enter when they feel threatened. In that state an animal's respiration and heartbeat slow; it lies limp and unresponsive, uninteresting to most predators who prefer to guarantee the freshness of their food by sinking their teeth into warm necks.

The possum in the road didn't move even after Samantha and I edged close enough to see its tongue hanging out, a little drool pooling at the corner of its open mouth. "It'd be no fun being dead," she observed matter-of-factly. But without a stethoscope, we couldn't know whether it was indeed dead or whether its heart was merely slowed while its ear, pressed into the dirt, translated the sounds of our sneakers to its brain in a command to stay low, stay frozen.

I do know possums aren't the only ones to hide inside their unhidden bodies. Some caterpillars clench themselves into tight, immovable balls. Giant water bugs and weevils lie inert in the face of danger. Hog-nosed snakes fake it. So do certain crickets and wasps.

And though I'm not heartened by the fact that a possum's brain is two hundred times smaller than a human's, I'm convinced there are times when its strategy is useful. "Just don't react!" I used to advise my twin when our older brother, a merciless tickler, would wrestle her to the living room rug and reduce her to that exquisite state between laughter and exhaustion. He'd long ago given up on me who could steel myself and look with disdain at his long fingers wiggling in the direction of my belly. We learn, I suppose, in various ways what to succumb to, what to resist. And if we choose the latter, we also learn whether to resist by fleeing or growing cold. Whether, in other words, to move our bodies or to remove our emotions.

In its own arachnid way, a male nursery web spider must wrestle with similar choices. Because its female counterpart walks a fine line between feelings of ardor and murder, he's likely to approach her with the gift of a delectable insect. If she's moved to eat it, he can begin to copulate. But if she, who isn't shy about munching the head of her mate, tires of the feast and turns her attention back to him, he's likely to collapse, fake a little death to preserve a little life.

Some humans do it too—fake our own deaths to avoid debt, prosecution, abusive marriages, revenge. Some of us attempt total erasure, which might mean starting over with a better nothing. Sometimes the hoax works; sometimes it doesn't.

A small-brained daddy longlegs has a better chance. Threatened, it can retract its long legs and lie motionless for half an hour, long enough for its predator to grow bored and wander off. A blue death-feigning beetle goes belly-up and rigid, and female robber flies fake it to avoid the amorous attention of a nearby male.

Imagine it: thousands of predators approach and thousands of critters flop over, curl into balls, tighten the body, slow their hearts, their breathings, slow time, slow the inevitable play-dead-or-be-eaten. I know this response well too—how to fake a little sleep now and then to avoid being bothered. How to hide inside the body, how to mute the *I'm available*—for sex or sustenance—signals while the body becomes its own crypt, a vault with a no trespassing sign.

And maybe no escape. For us introverts, that's the biggest risk: the danger of being stuck in our image of ourselves as strong, silent types. We begin to sink further into the image until the way out seems like too much work. Why not stay here a few days? Decades? Why not romanticize our reclusivity? Call ourselves monks in service to some higher calling?

When someone asked Mother Theresa what she said when she prayed, she replied, "I don't say anything. I just listen." And what, the person wanted to know, does God say to her? "God doesn't say anything. He listens."

I love the hope in silence her answer implies. I worry about it too. Taken to extremes, what's to prevent one from sliding into passivity, sinking into solipsistic determination to keep one's ear to one's own ear ad nauseam? Once the danger has passed, what's to lure us from the insular place that requires listening only to oneself, to one's own quiet, which might, in fact, be inbred and unhealthy?

Surely the answer for us humans is to examine our reasons for going mute, for acoustical camouflage, for thanatosis, for all the ways we might choose to insulate ourselves from external stimuli and work a while inside some container of quiet.

Everything, Rilke says,

> that has been wrestled from doubt,
> I welcome—the mouths that burst open after
> long knowledge of what it is to be mute.

But nothing musical is bursting open in me yet, so perhaps all this obsessive noodling is just a way to fool myself about performance. When I sit at home on the piano bench and imagine myself, half-hermit that I claim to be, in front of an audience with that Mozart piece in front of me, I have to admit that I, like so many other creatures afraid of being eaten alive, would likely freeze. Sometimes the only difference between a discerning audience and a foraging one is politeness. It's fear then, not any highfalutin notions of sacred space or cocoons of quiet, which seems finally reason enough to be self-protective. My hand's on the phone, ready to dial Betty's number, tell her I'm backing out.

And then the image of that possum grows vivid again. Thanatosis is a form of self-mimesis, meaning we imitate our dead selves, meaning we might be taking this not wanting to be heard to comic extremes. Or to tragic ones. One of the risks a possum runs is taking its "playing possum" role too seriously. Even as Samantha and I stood on the shoulder watching that motionless animal, choiceless, in the middle of the road that day, we could hear a car—the dirt and gravel spitting under its tires—approaching too fast, about to barrel around the bend.

16

Mile 20.5

UNDER THE MT. AETNA BRIDGE

———————

Forget denouements and falling action. Rivers sound more like songs sung in rounds: repetition, variation, staggered starts.

———————

Samantha picks up a stone from the bank by the bridge, names it "Little Princess in Jail," and throws it in the water. "So there," she yells.

———————

And so a basking painted turtle, likely feeling the vibration of ker-plunking stone or Samantha's boot on the bank, slides off a mossy log and plops into shallow water. Without vocal cords or outer ear, the species has survived for fifteen million years. Nearby leaf debris bobs up and down as water ripples from the turtle's point of entry.

17

Scales

One of my siblings is an architect; the other, an interior designer. On their rough sketches, they might note "NTS." *Not to scale.* It's a cautionary note: the space between windows might be narrower than it looks. Glancing at a sketch, a naïve client might fantasize about putting a cabinet there, big enough to hold place settings for twelve. But my siblings, who can visualize the negative space in a room, would stop their clients then and reemphasize: the sketches are *not to scale.* They'd point to that blank wall. See all this white space? It's deceptive. It'll shrink. Until the drawing of the space and its furnishings is done to scale, don't take it as an accurate representation.

They're saying, of course, that what the untrained eye sees on the drawings should not be trusted. Nor perhaps should the ear, especially among the bass-heavy music blaring from cars, the roar of planes, or the jabber we sometimes spew when we're threatened or bored. *NTS:* It's possible the noise itself has skewed the aural scale so much it doesn't represent the actual world.

These are up-on-the-ridge thoughts, triggered today by Samantha, who'd crawled into bed with us way before dawn and whispered into my back, "Meemi, when will we wake up?" Hers was a good question, in which I also heard one of mine: *Wake up to what?* After breakfast, with no good answer in mind, I had driven us up to what's known around here as "The Elbow," an almost three-thousand-foot-high overlook along the ridge of Big Savage Mountain. Below us, thousands of forested acres rise and fall in folded hills and creviced valleys, in shadows and light. In the deepest crease of them all runs the invisible, inaudible river.

"Remember yesterday, being down by the river? Way down there," I say to her, pointing. "That's where we were. Remember the crayfish we found?"

But she seems transfixed by the view, the miles and miles of deep green sweeping up and down ridges and valleys, stretching from here to West Virginia without a single sign of anything human but a power line. "Oh," she finally gasps, "it's the end of the world!" She often says something odd like that, and frequently we'll laugh, which used to make her cry. Today when I laugh, she seems proud, as if she knows that humor and wisdom can be compatible. Hers, though, are the songs of innocence, not experience, and, naturally, the next moment she's likely to say something ordinary or petty and to sound like the five-year-old she is, returned to her customary size.

Up here the panorama tests our responses to expansive scales. As in so many big places—prairies, deserts, seas—the view can make us feel small and insignificant. Whether that feeling threatens or consoles depends on our histories with claustrophobia—physical or emotional—and with horizons.

As babies, if we're lucky, our world begins as a looming breast, for weeks the only universe we know. If we're even luckier, the accompanying sounds are ones of suckle and coo, and the scale of baby to world is 1:1. Then we grow up and find beyond the breast a playground (1:15), a neighborhood (1:600), a village or city or farm. Forced to redefine our pleasures and our work, we might start to hear both the lullabies and battle cries of the world (1:7 billion) expanding from here—wherever we are—out into the universe where human ignorance and the silence of space (1:infinity) can terrify.

From this high point above the river today, I watch the sinuous crevice below wind toward Warnick's Point and then south to Peapatch Ridge. Thick forests shield the river from my sight, but I can imagine it twisting one way and then the other as it heads south toward the Potomac River, which runs southeast toward Chesapeake Bay and then out into the expansive Atlantic, the thousands of miles of watery gray from here to Portugal, up to the Canadian Maritimes, south to Tierra del Fuego, where not too long ago I'd rounded Cape Horn on a research boat and, a day later, sat across a table from a woman who said she knew a way to book passage on a Russian freighter headed that afternoon for Antarctica. The immediate question then was about money; the bigger one was how far I would go to hear what I imagine is cold silence. How much vastness could I, furless little animal with puny unmovable ears, stand?

I've lamented many times that for so many of us, the sounds of the places—big or small—where we live have become mere metaphor or muffled background noise. They seem to have less and less to do with us, who often don't wish to be distracted from ourselves while we elbow our way to center stage as if we could sustain ourselves as soloists. I understand the pleasure of being the singular focus of well-earned applause, but I worry about the accompanying danger of becoming groundless and wonder if that's what the speaker in Matthew Arnold's "Dover Beach" felt more than a hundred years ago. Standing at his own window looking across the sea—the English Channel, in his case—all he could hear was the sea as a *melancholy, long, withdrawing roar*. The end of faith, he thought. He had no sense of the tide as one of the most reliable reminders of rhythmical departures and returns, the consolation of repetitions, that what goes around usually comes around. In this love poem, he could hear, in other words, nothing but his own sadness. Such was the speaker's mood that night that I suspect even if some great white whale breeched or blew in the moonlight, he might have heard only the smack of a half-ton tail or the sputtering geyser of destruction on calm waters. *Doom*, he might have said. *Finis*. That's the nature of the inward-turning weight of personal sorrows. The question is for how long this turn and at what cost?

I should admit here that I'm drawn to the great stories of human longing. Paradoxically, they work on intimate scales and help us feel less alone. And I should confess, too, that when I'm angry or sad, I like to cling a while to any snippet of that fleeting story: *he said this and then he did that and—do you believe it?—he said it again!* At times like that I want the story to stay merely mine. And small, tiny enough, in fact, that I can carry it around for days or years, maybe make it part of who I am. Times, I acknowledge, when I wish to shrink the scale, be a soloist at the center of the universe. "But wait," a friend says, trying to soothe me. "Look at the big picture. Let's listen to the whole story." Though I know its value, I have, in wound-nursing times, hated that advice for the way it removes *me* as the measure of all things.

⎯⎯

How to live large one moment, small the next? How to adjust our sense of scale? Or how to live when the scale keeps shifting in spite of ourselves?

⎯⎯

Two days before I considered Antarctica, I'd been part of a group lucky enough to disembark at Cape Horn, climb the narrow path to the top of the cliff, and look out over that notorious "end of the world." The storms there are historic, punctuated by rogue waves and williwaw winds. Rounding the Horn in 1832, Darwin wrote in his diary that he was haunted by the sounds of peril—the booms and crash of surf on stone, which, legend claims, can be heard a full twenty miles inland. It was Darwin, of course, who managed the second major adjustment of scale, revealed us as an ongoing part of a long chain of evolution. He and Galileo, that first adjuster who'd earlier removed us from the center of the universe, began to dismantle a different sort of peril: that self-congratulatory notion that we, just by the virtue of being human, are innately significant. Up on that Cape Horn cliff, the roar of wind drowns out almost everything else. It's not just more possible there to think of something other than one's own life: it's unavoidable. Immensities loom to the south and west and east, and under the surface of the roiling seas teem not just the kingdoms of marine life but the graveyards of the galleons and tankers that flailed here and failed.

Evolution can't console, so it's no wonder sailors carried Bibles with them, no wonder that there on the cliff at the end of the world someone had built a small chapel and fastened it sturdily to the stone. On the day I was there, a small boy sat inside with his head bowed. I don't know where he came from or what he prayed for—salvation, I suppose, something other than the end of the world, which, for many, necessitates prayer.

How else to live with the sound of our own insignificance?

———

In the Mozart piece I've been working on for months, the right hand runs up and down scales and arpeggios, the high notes light as small chimes or tinkling ice. "Like that?" I ask Betty, who can glance at the notes and hear in an instant how the whole line should sound.

She nods.

What the left hand ought to do is quietly anchor the right, provide a stable, lower, repeating four-note pattern. But I can't control my left thumb. It's loutish, lumpish. Every time I try to lower it gently, it thuds on the key, banging that one bass note so heavily the relative dynamics between treble and clef are reversed, which means the melody is momentarily drowned out.

"Lighter with the left," she keeps reminding me. "Lighter!"

Isn't that the broader dilemma too? How, as they say, to walk lightly? Or how to keep our justified stomping—about injustice, cruelties, the various wrongs we might try to right—from drowning out the likes of music, birdsong, our gestures of ordinary kindness?

"Practice, practice," Betty would insist. "Try it softer here, louder there."

Or, my siblings might suggest, "Rescale the drawings."

There, I think; that must be a piece of it: counter all that vastness we shrink from with intimacy. Get back to the details. For me, up on the ridge today with my present preoccupation, that means getting back to the sounds down by the river far below: snake hissing, beaver slapping, water gurgle, and rumble of rock. And other sounds I can almost imagine: the crayfish in the river near our feet the other day. Not just the slurp of its emergence from muddy bank but the sudden scurry back when it sensed danger, including the giant, sun-obliterating shadow my own body made.

———

Up on the overlook Samantha, evidently bored, has plunked herself down on a big flat stone and taken to chewing the ends of her pigtails. Around us the air's grown even quieter. "The snow has stopped," we say. "The rain is over." But the wind, we say, "has died." There's even a word for a dead wind: *anasilan*, the Gothics called it, as if a breeze or gale could just keel over, begin to rot, like the possum we saw down there last month that might by now have ceased to stink.

I'm not one to dwell on doomsday, but *dead wind* pricks a worry about the end of *something* I can't quite name. Up here at Samantha's "end of the world," I fret about her generation's slow detachment. I don't know how much to blame the iPhones and video games they seem so tethered to, but if they and future generations drift away from a world whose myriad critters—including us—depend, at least in part, on seeing what's conspicuous and half-hidden, hearing both clear notes and innuendoes, how will they know the relationship between quiet and clamor is often awry? Or understand relationships between parts and the whole? How will they achieve—whatever their fields—what Betty and my siblings have sometimes achieved: the ability to infer from partial clues—sketches and scores—a final entirety, a bigger picture?

———

And so I've kept at it, practicing those Mozart measures, hearing the melody note one day and not the next, until one afternoon last week, as my left thumb clunked, I heard immediately what I wasn't hearing. *That*, I think, is what has to happen. We have to know what we're missing. Just as stargazers in the city miss the night sky, we noise-bombarded folks will have to miss the sounds of the larger, natural world. Or as my siblings might say: given that we mostly live by not-to-scale sketches, we must learn to imagine what doesn't seem present.

This is not about spirits or ghosts. It is, I see now, about imagining ourselves *simultaneously* up on the ridge and down by the river. The challenge isn't so much about comfort with large scales or small but about flexibility, the mind being nimble enough to move from expanse to minutiae, to hear that vast silence even as we cherish whatever versions of suckle and coo can nourish us still.

———

I didn't book a berth on that Russian freighter to Antarctica, haven't yet agreed to that flirtation with the steeper spans of silence and space that might tell me more than I want to know. But others have, and I've needed them, those wanderers across the planets and galaxies, the Shackletons and Armstrongs, Amelia Earharts, even Captain Jean-Luc Picard on the *Enterprise*—those tiny figures leaving their small houses and crossing wide waters, empty ice, the blackness of space. And those wanderers across the imagination: Shakespeare, the Buddha, Rilke, who claims, *This is how he grows: by being defeated, decisively, / by constantly greater beings*.

Oh, there'll be time again for the soloists, for Mozart and Einstein, all those soaring accomplishments and accompanying sounds we humans have made, other days to praise the hum and eurekas of progress that have saved millions of lives and eased the travails of millions more.

Samantha, meanwhile, is about to toss her shoes off the edge of the cliff. When I nix that idea, saying we'd never find them, she maintains, poutily, that all we'd have to do is go down there. It'd be easy. "See?" she says, pointing below. "We just walk until we're right under these rocks, and then we look down, and there they'll be!"

From up here, a child can't imagine a shoe getting lost down there in all that leafy green or the need to bushwhack through miles of rhododendron thickets as the forest closes in, leaving us searchers without landmark or signpost until soon it would not just be the shoes we were hunting but some way home. Nor can a young child imagine a self getting lost. But we can. It's why, I suspect, we have to keep repositioning ourselves along the scale, doing the work, at least now and then, that makes us big enough to be seen or heard, even in a world, we'd better learn, that's full of the chomp and song of eat and mate, then birth and death, ad infinitum for millennia, and most of it without us.

———

Retying her shoes, I remember the sky, infinite blue vault like this one, high over the fields of my childhood, the source, I used to think, of some music of the spheres. Never mind the innocence of that notion. Or of the transcendence Loren Eiseley refers to when he says, *Surely he [humans] came because he is at heart a listener, and a searcher for some transcendental realm beyond himself.* Eiseley was an archaeologist. The transcendental realm to which he listened was, ironically, subterranean, reached, shovel by trowel, through geologic eons and humans' early history. We can't, in his profession, know who we are until we know where we've been. And today I add: and until we know what we are *among*—the whole intimacy and scope of it. Sightings help, as do soundings—in both meanings of the word: how we measure depths and what we listen to.

The more accurate aural scales must be able to handle the range. Whatever the acoustical equivalent of the scales my siblings use, without *some* sliding sense of scale, we don't know if we're hearing ourselves and others as main characters in a haiku or an epic, in a family history or the universal/galactic story that science has been unearthing—uncosmosing—more and more. How, finally, to understand the scale of our own stories in relation to larger ones? How to keep, simultaneously, one ear to the human heart and one ear cocked to the neighborhood, the past, the planet, the future?

My siblings would say that if you ignore an *NTS* warning and use a rough sketch to build your kitchen anyway, it's likely things won't work out as you'd imagined. The room might be functional, but something will seem out of alignment—the sink area too squished, the gap between fridge and backdoor too wide. To expand the metaphor—perhaps that's what it takes to know the scale by which we've been living by might be woefully inaccurate: a sense of overcrowding or, equally likely, of emptiness. Or both, simultaneously. And perhaps that, to revise Samantha's earlier question, is what we might wake up to. Or won't.

18

Mile 22

NEAR CAREY RUN

The spiritual: our needs, our longings, the come and go of them. But the river endures. It's here, even while it goes.

"The silence of the in between," Samantha says, "is yellow."

Maybe we learn the song from the mourning dove but the meaning of its song from somewhere else?

"I used to think," she says, "that adults were smart."

And then there's the sound of acorns dropping. *Plink* if they're ripe, full of nut; *tap* if they're hollow, the nut unformed. The *plinks* outnumber the *taps* this season, which means the squirrels will survive and the bears will have their fill and fewer of either species will bang on bird feeders in late winter.

19

Practicing

It isn't instinct that's led me out of the house this morning and into this snowstorm alone, dressed in triple layers, hat, and gloves. It might by now be a habit, but if so, it's habit that began with a choice, which, like many choices, prompts a little musing. Today is another weekly stream-monitoring day, and because my sometimes companions are elsewhere, I have more time to think about how, if at all, these small efforts matter. How does stream monitoring help to stem the call to drill, the lure of money, the gas industry's promise of cleaner energy or whatever other worrisome short-term fixes we're inclined to pursue? I know the obvious answer: the scientific data we send to state agencies might someday show that something's contaminating the river, which might then trigger investigations, testimony, protests against the intrusion of trucks and wells and too many chain saws and all that. It's the less obvious answer I'm after today.

In the meantime, regular walks along the Savage River led me last week to start reading about snow and sound, so today this river in a blizzard has become something more than it used to be. It is, in fact, the sound of millions of tiny air bubbles exploding as they smash into stones and underwater logs. And snow falling into the river? If crayfish had keen enough ears—or ears at all—they'd hear each flake ding as it hits the water: more explosions of air bubbles, more evanescent detonations. *Chahatlin*, the Inuit call it: snow that sizzles on water. Auditory reminders are everywhere— chafe, scuff, scour; we live in a world of constant collision, plenty of opportunities to test our limits, if we need to, to scrape against the corral that corrals us—physically, mentally. How else would we know whether we can scale walls or leap chasms, and if we find we can, whether the choice to do so is courageous or foolish?

Mistakes, of course, are inevitable.

My blacksmith friend reminds me that sooner or later every blacksmith goes too far: thins copper beyond its limits and watches the hammer punch a hole right through it; cools a piece of steel too quickly and ends up banging it in half. The trick, he tells me, is to listen to the sound of hammer on metal. How close to the metal's limits are you? How soon before one more whack rips in two a piece you'd pictured as a single, sinuous curve? The sounds of collision can be subtle—ping versus thunk, creak versus ring. The better you hear them, the more you can shape and design. He's talking metal; I'm hearing *life*.

And I'm thinking about Hephaestus, that lowly Greek god of metalworking who walks, as does my friend, with a limp, who's learned, as has my friend, that limits—and the choice to yield to or try to transcend them—help shape who we are.

⌇

Thickening snow lowers the sky—white above and below, ahead and behind. I could be anywhere in this storm, plastic cup in one hand, and in the other, a thirty-inch metal rod curved into a loop on one end. The tool, made by my blacksmith friend, is ingenious: when I reach the river in a few minutes, it will allow me to stand safely on the bank, slip the cup in the loop, lean over without risk of falling in, and scoop the water I need to determine temperature, conductivity, and total dissolved solids—the markers we're tracking in case fracking starts to sully these waters.

I let the metal rod drag beside me, make a tiny trail beside the footsteps I might need to follow back to my car. Except for the faint ripple of river ahead somewhere in the blur and the soft flump of my boots, all else seems silent. But here again is how attentiveness—perhaps taken to the absurd—can enliven the mundane:

Like the river, fresh snow is full of air pockets, which means I'm walking through something like a giant, cold version of those bounce houses Samantha and her sister like to jump in. All that air in the snow is why if you take a spill in a storm, you'll likely stand right back up, brush off your pants, continue on. There's no frozen ground to crunch against, no icy overlay to bruise a knee. Nothing to stop you—especially if you're alone—from flopping down on your back to make angels in the snow, longingly, as if such a flat-on-your-back dance could make you believe again. It's tempting to think nothing's limiting you. Nobody's watching. In fact, here, where the strictures of good sense might seem suspended, nobody could report your antics even if he or she wanted to. Sound, it turns out, is as dampened as your usual decorum. Even the deer snorts I might hear here are muffled, trapped among and within the zillions of flakes that thicken the air, pile up underfoot.

I could have used a little muffling last week. At the end of more than two years of practice, after months of Betty's tempered praise—"It's getting there"; "It's coming along"—I finally sat down at the piano in front of a small audience. Betty likes a bit of formality first. "Tell us," she said, "a little about the piece you're going to play." I said nothing about those evenings I've sat at home with the lights off, Mitsuko Uchida on the CD player, her interpretation of the second movement beautifully juxtaposing the haunting melancholy and nuanced repetitions that remind me that our habits—often limiting but necessary—can, if we're lucky, deepen into endless variations.

Instead I mentioned Mozart's canary and the trills in this sonata, and all the while I could feel the tension in my shoulders clump down my arm. I repositioned myself on the stool, fanned out my fingers, pulled my shoulders down, and took a deep breath. But within ten measures, I'd botched the arpeggios, found and discarded the rhythms, underplayed what should have been accented, and clunked what I wanted to be graceful. I heard, in other words, a different kind of pang: something lovely getting mangled. Within four minutes I could also hear someone's nervous cough and the rub of fabric against chair as people squirmed. How, I wondered—six minutes in and quite detached now from whatever those plank-like hands were doing down there at the ends of my arms—could I slink off the stool, slither under the piano and out the back door I'd already noted wasn't tightly closed? The rest of the details don't matter—the polite applause, Betty's small smile and silence—for this isn't a story about performance but about banging against one's limits and hearing them hold, about examining illusions, signing off as a soloist, sloughing Orpheus from the mythos of me.

———

"Congratulations," the stranger beside me whispered. We were standing in New Jersey's Brigantine Wildlife Refuge, taking turns at a high-powered scope trained on a snowy owl on the far side of a slough of brackish water. Rarely seen here, the owl perched on a small rise of reeds and grasses like a dignified statue of feathers and hollow bones, the epitome of deliberate silence. It can swivel its head 180 degrees, but on that day it stood stock still, taking stock, it seemed to me, of this gaggle of humans peering into scopes, whispering excitedly.

Congratulations? What had I done to merit that? I turned to look at him.

"Your first snowy, right?"

I nodded.

"Congratulations," he repeated, bending to peer through his scope again.

This is birder talk, quest talk, the talk of life listers who study habitats, migratory patterns, who know this influx of snowy owls in South Jersey—the biggest in almost a hundred years—has something to do with the dwindling supply of lemmings farther north. I admire the way their passion intertwines with knowledge and a taste for trekking on cold days like this one, but did the man think I was one of them? That I'd been following birding posts and blogs all week, had arisen at dawn, driven miles to get here, where sightings had been reported?

The truth is I was there only because I'd needed a break from teaching a memoir workshop at a nearby conference. Tired of seesawing between criticism and support, I'd gotten in the car at lunchtime and driven north a few miles to where someone said you could get out and walk, breathe a little salty air. I just happened, in other words, to be at the right place at the right time.

Still, the owl was there and so was I, and in spite of what I know about talons and beaks and the soft bellies of lemmings, I felt good about my luck, about seeing that dignified stillness positioned like some kind of marble out there in the decaying marsh. Its beauty reminded me, as the Elgin marble had reminded Keats, of the limits of mortality, weakened spirits, and wasted time.

And so I'm back to this: Given all those limits, does it even matter that I'm trying to figure out how to care about the planet, especially since I, privileged as I am, lazy as I can be, like the comfort of a warm bed on winter mornings? Should I say *that* to the birder beside me? But nothing in the salty air that day invited personal stories. We were there, a dozen of us, unrecognizable in face-wrapped scarves and hoodies, speaking in hushed tones because out there in the marsh was an Arctic raptor. And because such moments are rare, we talked, if we talked at all, in whispers. Regardless of how we'd ended up there—choice or happenstance—we had the sense that being there meant turning down the volume, and so the raptor stayed.

———

I don't know why certain sounds—wind chimes on the back porch, loon calls, that big owl's silence—can open an ache in me. I only know—at least for the moment—that today's steady hiss of snow on snow works like a *psst* in my ear, making the mundane both more mundane and less: *mundus*, after all, means *the world*. Which is why Hephaestus is my man of the day. Hephaestus, not singing his way into a heavenly future but crafting a doable way into the palpable present. Homer says the gods honored him as their wounded workman. His language would have included the likes of *rivet*, *weld*, and *wedge*, the verbs, in other words, of joining, binding, fixing in place, the ring of metal on metal, those repeated dings of small adjustments, pressure and patience—*it's getting there*—the clang of reshaping, the long steady practice that yields, perhaps one out of ten times, the perfectly shaped bowl.

I'm trying to see what it's like, in other words, not just to practice but *to have a practice*. I'd like to reach a point where the choice to sit at the piano or go for a walk is less and less a choice and more and more simply what I do. Progress is gratifying, of course: a permanent ban on drilling matters, and a decent piano performance might be fun. But until then spending a little time every day with music and wandering the watershed with an ear to the river might eventually become a habit, like something one wears, not so much a garment but skin, part of the body. Habit then might deepen to *inhabit*, to dwell in a place, maybe even a life. I'd like that.

In the meantime, I admit there's something comic about trudging in a blizzard like a penitent with a cup in hand or about any number of other practices we humans have adopted, especially in a world where solipsism and waste are out of control and the impact of such practices is likely limited. But there are, I want to believe, fewer limits to how we might someday reimagine our lives. And recognizing absurdity might be part of that. The word *absurd* itself comes from the Latin *absurdus*, from *ab* and *surdus*, meaning deaf, insensible. I like this ancient association, its suggestion that when the world and our lives seem absurd, it might partially be because the ear we've turned to them has grown deaf. Reason enough, it seems to me, to keep up whatever practice might retune us a little more finely.

⌒⌒

Out of the blizzardy blur, the river finally emerges—dark, cold, close to its source a few miles away, and therefore clean, for now. And here at its most accessible point, totally frozen. I trudge back and forth along the bank ten feet, twenty, listening for any trickle that means a thinner layer of ice and a chance of breaking through to the water. A ways downstream from the shadowy hemlocks, I finally hear muffled ripples, slip down the bank, inch one foot out onto the snow-covered ice, lift the blunt end of the steel rod high, and ram it hard against the surface, which cracks but doesn't open. Again and again, I ram it, the collision reverberating up my arm, rattling my teeth.

It's tempting here to think about analogies: what I might or might not tell Samantha someday about punching holes in our armors, the pleasure of turning this whole effort into some metaphor about accepting the limits of one's strength or perseverance, at the very least one's choice to be out and about in a blizzard. But what happens next is both unresonant sound—a higher-pitched thud of metal against ice—and literal image: my awareness of me as a mere speck in the blizzard, one boot on the bank, ice cracking beneath the other, and that sudden surge of strength. At the moment of limits testing, no matter how lofty or mundane, isn't that the rush? We push harder, jump higher, ram harder because we long to surpass—even momentarily—our usual selves.

Of course what comes after that must be some version of what, indeed, comes after that: my boot plunges through, and icy water soaks my socks. Scrambling back to the bank, I squat on what I'm pretty sure is the firm edge, wedge the clear plastic cup into the loop of metal and extend it as far as I can over the ice and through the hole my boot has just made. Frost's poem "Directive" comes to mind and its image of the speaker with a child's goblet and the stream he has managed, at last, to find. *Here are your waters*, Frost says, *and your watering place. / Drink and be whole again beyond confusion.*

Lowering the cup into the water, I suspect that wholeness, too, is an illusion, unless by wholeness we mean that fleeting moment that fills us with a longing far larger than what we've conceived of as our limits. From there it's a choice: live nostalgically in that moment—perhaps for the rest of our lives—or let it galvanize us into what might soon become a practice, maybe even second nature: the regular hammering and shaping of, if not the perfect bowl, then maybe a song or a meal, at the very least a petition or protest—something, however small, with whatever limited results, that might begin to protect whatever it is we love. That—not perfection—is what practice might make.

20

Polyphony

A single sound is but a vanity, a betrayal of communion and community.
RUSSELL SHERMAN

At first I want to argue with Russell Sherman's claim. Just listen to Judy Collins or any number of other soloists whose sound is pure, singular. It's not that their voices do or do not betray any sense of community or communion; it's that they, for the moment, seem to make community irrelevant. It's you and me and the music, the singer says; the rest of the world recedes. It's possible, in moments like those, to feel, as they say, blissfully lost in song.

At least that's what I was thinking one winter night just after I left a Collins concert and made my way down the cacophony of Fifth Avenue in Manhattan.

But today three hundred miles to the south, in Finzel Swamp, where Samantha's stalking mud puddles and I've been listening to a wood thrush, I'm in the mood for reconsiderations. Something about this high valley in western Maryland has me rethinking the tension between individual and community—what's lost or gained when allegiances shift or don't to something larger than oneself. Here, near the headwaters of the Savage River, sound reverberates from one sedgy clump to another, as well as up and down from surrounding hills to treetops to the tangles of emergent grasses. In other words, not just bird sounds trigger my reconsiderations. It's those familiar sounds against the backdrop of ancient ooze that's got me thinking again about Sherman's claim. And I'm not feeling lost but, oddly, quite at home.

An old house once stood at the far edge of this swamp, another one up the hill a bit, and a newer one on the western edge. All three are gone now, as are the big culverts under the dirt road that once carried cars over the water. The road is gone too, along with the wolves and elk and a group of men who used to play hockey on the frozen pond to the north. The dirt road's been replaced by a wet footpath that winds like a corridor between highbush blueberry and twisted alder and everywhere the dark water seeps, much of it choked with skunk cabbage and watercress. You have to want hard to come here now, and there's no invitation to stay. This is not a community, in other words, that opens its swampy arms, makes it easy for you to say "home."

Yet "home" is how it feels.

Bending down, Samantha and I twirl our twigs through a puddle. My twig, trailing a wake of cloudy brown, intersects with hers. They muddy the water. Narcissus would have had a different life here. Without a clear pool, he couldn't have gotten stuck in self-absorption and the interminable replication of his own image. Maybe here he would have been simply stuck in the mud. And from there, who knows? Perhaps being rooted in a single place might have made him decide to look around, pay more attention—not to himself but to where he was. Or maybe, in the myth's defense, that's what transformation—his, ours—sometimes takes: increasing boredom with a small self and a wish at last to move on to something larger. The questions then would be, How long would *that* take? And do we have time?

Samantha, whose sense of time is usually like that of most five-year-olds—immediate or nonexistent—stands up and skips down to a larger puddle where one boot and then the other adds a two-beat stomp to the contrast between the slurp of swamp and the flute-like song of a wood thrush. It's that contrast that nags at me and complicates my notions of community and self and whether our sense of the latter can ever seem complete.

Because the wood thrush repeats his phrases—*ee-o-lay, ee-o-lay*—we can think we've heard the whole song, beginning to end. If I were to graph the sound, I could mark discrete stops and starts, have some confidence that I'm hearing the entire phrase, that there's nothing, aurally at least, that's eluding me. There's a certain satisfaction in expressions with clear beginnings and ends. A politician promises better industry regulations, and we check his or her name on the ballot and go home. There, we like to say, putting away our boots and petitions, that's done.

But of course it's not.

Nothing's ever finished. Here and elsewhere, there are always subtle currents and sideways slips, the half-hidden undergrowth, things about to emerge from dark water. If we hear swamp sounds at all, we don't expect to hear them as phrases. Their murmur is continuous, undulating without closure, a muted milieu destined to confound any notion of completion. No wonder we treasure the birdsong, the slogan, or some identifiable sound of the self—voice, breath, the thump of our own heart. Those sounds can have an aural form, shaped and discrete. Their familiarity can comfort, even if we know their completeness is, paradoxically, made more complete because there's always the backdrop of a bigger world in constant flux.

And it's not just the stable phrase in a mutable setting that complicates a sense of self. There's also the pull of future and past on the present. Behind us the wood thrush's song almost erases the long brutal winter we've just come through. It's the sound of new and now, of fresh, of bright green beginnings.

But all around, mud gives way beneath my boot, the ooze reminding me that this wet valley is an ancient one, a refugium where boreal species—tamaracks and cotton grass—from further north were trapped during the last ice age.

In other words, I know the bird's solo will not last. In a few months he'll be gone, his short stay here juxtaposed against the background of timelessness: the one ephemeral life made more singular and therefore more poignant by what endures around it.

To listen to the bird alone, then, is to have one's ear tuned to a specific singing creature for a certain proscribed time. But to listen to the bird in a swamp is also to have one's ear pulled out and away in an open-ended expansiveness.

It isn't a question, finally, of which sounds—the bird's or the swamp's—bring more pleasure or whether, as Russell Sherman says, the single sound "betrays" the community. The question is more complex: Can I properly hear both at the same time?

And that, I see at last, is what Betty has been trying to teach me. "Listen orchestrally," she often says. Back at the piano, a few weeks after my disappointing performance, I was trying to play a little Bach while she was trying to help me think about the varieties of musical sound a single chord can convey. Think flute: trapeze dancing. Think cello: slow river sighing. Think, I say to myself this afternoon, following Samantha down the trail, of the kinglet's *tee tee tee, tew tew ti-dadee*, wind in the willows, voices of family, whine of chain saw, protests of the powerless.

If we were to think more orchestrally, we could still appreciate the breathtaking solos, Collins, for sure, and Pavarotti, the geniuses like Mozart and Bach, the simple eloquence of Mandela or Gandhi. And certainly there's the possibility that each of us might, in our own small lives, have a few solo moments of transcendence while appreciative audiences applaud. But given that those heights are not sustainable, what about thinking of ourselves—of all beings— as part of some community orchestra, still tuning our instruments, warming up, so to speak?

I know I could love the idea that birds and frogs, for example, have evolved in such a way that their songs and croaks don't overlap acoustically. Sound is organized into aural niches, which, as one theory goes, makes the critters more likely to attract mates and protect themselves. I imagine all of us introverts would covet such an even divvying up of acoustical space. I worry, though, about the tidiness and inherent optimism of any neat arrangement, about whether that niche theory is but a different version of that old celestial chorus brought down to earth. The world—acoustical, visual, physical, spiritual—is messier than that.

———

So, sometimes, is Bach. Especially his fugal work in *The Well-Tempered Clavier*. I listened to parts of it last week, played the recordings over and over, trying to do what one's supposed to do with such polyphonic music: tease the strands apart. It sounded at first like mishmash. But by the fifth or sixth time, I'd begun to hear the subject in the bass separate from both countersubjects in the treble, all of them traveling along in C minor, so if I closed my eyes and concentrated, I could hear three voices at once, all of them moving together and separately through time. What had been acoustical blur began to transform into discrete voices, none of which tries to accommodate the others or to move up or down an interval to create harmonies. It was as if all three strands of music were going about their own acoustical lives, the pluralities of which add up to a masterpiece.

Here in the swamp, trying to listen that way means going back and forth between the whole and its multiple inhabitants until even the back-and-forth dissolves and what emerges is this small, acoustically enacted truth: there's delicate space among even the seemingly undifferentiated stuff of the world. Just as that subject in Bach's bass is not the countersubject in the treble, a sparrow is not a wren, and a marsh wren is not a house wren, and one of the ways you can tell the difference is by the rattle at the end of the former one's song. By extension, to the uninitiated a turkey gobble might sound like a deer snort; a Bach bourrée, like a Mozart minuet. To the initiated, though, you might as well be comparing a hammering downpour to a tree-dripping drizzle. The point is not that we all should be experts on birdsong or Bach; it's that hearing fine aural distinctions can make what seems at first a cacophony of indistinct songs separate into fourteen different species. Which is to know that attentive discernments unblur the world and layer it deep.

And old.

If we include in this polyphony the voices from the past, then we can imagine hearing today's thrush song, along with the long-gone wolf howl and elk snort, the far-past grind of glaciers to the north. Push this even further: If the planet continues to warm, then today's slurp of swamp will turn dry and crunchy; the alders will die, the frogs will depart for damper ground, and the heron who likes its feet wet will take its *kuck-kuck* and fly elsewhere. If we hear landscape as polyphonic across space and time, then we might better anticipate the future sound of rising sea levels, slowed-to-a-trickle streams, the roar of flame (they're already flaring fracked gas in North Dakota), or pound of drill.

Of course, change happens all the time. The mastodon and dodo bird are gone, along with thousands of other species. Ice ages begin and end; the climate warms and cools. But no natural processes match the speed with which these changes are happening now; no one knows what creatures, including us, will be able to adapt. And so the question climatologists now ask, with increasing urgency, is, How fast and with what consequences?

I'd like to enlarge the picture: If—as many speculate—the world's environmental problems are partly the result of a failure of imagination, then I would argue that an undeveloped acoustical imagination is part of that failure too. One possible solution: learning to hear our stories as solos in the thick of an urgently present now and, simultaneously, as part of an older community drama.

———

The thrush has stopped singing, and over to the east somewhere a bird I don't recognize is belting out a song I don't know. Further along the trail Samantha has flopped down on a low bridge, and just on the other side of the tussock I hear a sudden splash I can't account for. No wonder this place feels so mysteriously like home. It's all so audibly, palpably *here*—the amorphous and the discrete, the unanswerable and answerable, the paradoxical tensions we might someday learn to live with.

Sherman, I see now, wants us to understand that the betrayal he decries isn't the single note itself but the stopping there—because to stop there, enthralled, is to disallow the larger possibilities. The key is to hear that single note as a beginning, a sound made more beautiful when it's combined with others—in chords, sonatas, symphonies. A community of sound, sometimes intensely intimate, in which, for a short while we might feel blissfully lost, which might also feel like home. It's a true comfort for me to spend a little time like this, belly flat on the low bridge, saying not much at all while Samantha dangles the tips of her long hair toward the water. Surely what we ultimately need is both large and small intimacies, even as, inevitably, the world intrudes—television's horrific images, the radio's bad news, or just the discordant hum of inequality making different people hear different things. To paraphrase Robert Frost: Something there is that wants our lives to be more complicated than we wish.

In musical terms what Bach composed, in other words, was a way of listening to multiple voices.

Back home, I'll sit at the piano again or study the fugue or pull on boots and head downriver to the monitoring sites. But for an hour or so here, I'll listen, turn my head this way or that, try to follow the wood thrush's song, the horned owl's hoot, the sudden splash of a wood duck, a few unexplained rattles and chips. None of this will answer the bigger questions, and none of this will be sufficient.

But if there's solace here at the headwaters of the Savage River, it's not only because these headwaters and its critters are aesthetically pleasing to me but also because the place seems like a truer kind of home, meaning the way things are—squishy and polyphonic. Here and now—in this opened space, among these songs and wails, strums and snarls, that might have little to do with one another or with whatever small complaint or cheer I might myself at the moment be harrumphing—*here* there might be room for all of it. And for us, who try to find a way to live in this wildly wounded world by sometimes covering our ears, closing our eyes, trudging silently along, who sometimes sing to one another, sometimes hover between song and aimless hum. Room, too, for the unknown and dissonant, for the incongruities of our lives, and for a child who hands you a heart she's scrawled with a purple crayon. Though she can't yet know the connection between purple hearts and wartime wounds, she said to me last week, "When your heart touches your heart, sometimes it hurts." And now, as the wood thrush resumes his *ee-o-lay* and a tendril of emerald slime drifts under the bridge, I hear in her comment both our history—bleak and triumphant— and a strangely hopeful accuracy.

21

Mile 29

AT THE HEADWATERS

―――――〜〜〜――――

The swampy headlands of the Savage are engorged with the biological, which means steeped in webs of profusion and brutality and soaked in a little of this, a little of that. Undiagrammable. Here, grammar is either a joke or illusion. Prepositions sound less like *next*, more like *next to, next to*.

Listening only for sounds at the expense of story is often insufficient, but listening only for story can multiply what I'm missing.

Or is the storyline so flattened here it's more radial than melodic? Splat. Every footstep squishes into three directions; every plan oozes into six.

―――――〜〜〜――――

"There's an ear inside an ear," Samantha said once, giggling.

―――――〜〜〜――――

All the while, *conkeree* and *coo* of blackbird and dove, small gurgle of rivulet over half-submerged log, rustle of reeds, marsh wren chip, frog kerplunk, and everywhere and nowhere the slow slurp of water and earth in the act of trading places.

―――――〜〜〜――――

Names for each and for each of us, but no name yet for the whole shebang. *World?* Too abstract. *Home?* Lacks discernment. How about *Here and there and all the while?* Words that carry, as words can do, the sound of expansion, the flap of billowed-out walls and lifted ceilings, a sense of space widening. The mourning dove on the nearby branch is also twenty miles away, as are the dangers and hopes of what we call progress. The world stretches from under my foot clear to the far horizon; space triples, and soon it seems that like a river's one necessity, the whole scene's on the verge of merging into the next bigger one, which is the nature of emptying.